Monologues for Actors of Color

Women

"Actors—these voices will fly off the page into performance. Inspired! Relevant! Now!"

Kamilah Forbes, *Artistic Director, Hi-Arts/Hip Hop Theater Festival*

"These ferocious literary voices inspire me, intimidate me, empower my pen, and smash open my expectations of what a play can be. They provide gifts for actors, in the form of complex characters and throbbing language. I'm thrilled to share the page with them."

Quiara Alegría Hudes, *Pulitzer Prize Winning Playwright*

"Every actor needs something to play. This book on a practical level gives actors of many different backgrounds additional material for going out there and giving it their all."

Anna Deavere Smith, *Playwright and Actor*

Actors of color need the best speeches to demonstrate their skills and hone their craft. Roberta Uno has carefully selected monologues that represent African-American, Native American, Latino, Asian-American, and other identities. Each monologue comes with an introduction and notes on the characters and stage directions to set the scene for the actor.

This new edition includes some of the most exciting and accomplished playwrights to have emerged over the 15 years since the *Monologues for Actors of Color* books were first published—from new, cutting edge talent to Pulitzer prize-winners.

Roberta Uno is a theater director and dramaturg. She founded the New WORLD Theater and is the Director of Arts in a Changing America at the California Institute of the Arts.

Monologues for Actors of Color
Women

SECOND EDITION

Edited by Roberta Uno
Assistant Editor Margaret Odette

Routledge
Taylor & Francis Group

LONDON AND NEW YORK

Second edition published 2016
by Routledge
2 Park Square, Milton Park, Abingdon, Oxon OX14 4RN

and by Routledge
711 Third Avenue, New York, NY 10017

Routledge is an imprint of the Taylor & Francis Group, an informa business

First edition published by Routledge 2000

British Library Cataloguing-in-Publication Data
A catalogue record for this book is available from the British Library

Library of Congress Cataloguing-in-Publication Data
A catalog record for this book has been requested

ISBN: 978-1-138-85727-8 (hbk)
ISBN: 978-1-138-85728-5 (pbk)
ISBN: 978-1-315-71879-8 (ebk)

Typeset in Helvetica and Gill Sans
by Book Now Ltd, London

Dedicated to the legacy of New WORLD Theater
...and for Mikiko

Contents

Preface

This new edition of *Monologues for Actors of Color: Women*, and a companion collection for men, places in your hands some of the most original, fierce, funny, provocative, and moving writing available to actors seeking to inhabit characters as diverse and fascinating as the United States of America in the twenty-first century.

Two decades have passed since I was prompted by a symposium entitled, "Training the Actor of Color," at New York University's Tisch School of the Arts, to research and edit the original edition of this book. At that gathering in 1994, gifted acting students of color lamented their peripheral existence in major training programs, both as numerical minorities and as minor characters in the majority of works produced. Although they were enthusiastic about color-blind casting, they also passionately advocated for greater opportunities to speak through the lens of their racial, ethnic, and gender identities. While some drama programs continue to lag behind, forward-thinking institutions and arts organizations are forging a wider American theater. Margaret Odette, assistant editor of this volume and a graduate student in NYU's MFA Acting Program, notes change as a member of a class that is now comprised of 50 percent people of color, "This is an empowering time to be an actor of color—because more institutions are embracing us and promoting our success in equal measure with white artists, creating a more dynamic and enriching artistic experience for everyone. The American theater is finally starting to catch up with the world that we as artists are charged with the task of reflecting, and we all benefit as a result."

What was once a project of multicultural inclusion has now become a forecast of a new, polycultural America, one that has been artistically revitalized by a stunning array of voices, aesthetics and narratives. Beyond the walls of the theater, the country has changed in ways that challenge US theaters and training programs to find greater relevance to current and future audiences. The United States is experiencing unprecedented, dramatic demographic change. The US Census Bureau has projected that by the year 2042, for the first time, there will be no single racial or ethnic majority in a growing country of 439 million. And this change will occur much earlier, by 2023, for the nation's children under 18. The shift to an aggregated majority of people of color—African Americans, Latinos, Asian Americans, Native Americans, and multi-racial Americans—has already occurred in many locations from major metros like New York City, to entire states including California, Hawai'i, New Mexico, and Texas.

The production and recognition of diverse playwrights has also greatly increased in the last two decades. For example, the decade prior to 1994 saw only two Pulitzer Prizes for Drama awarded to a sole playwright of color: August Wilson in 1987 and again in 1990. There were four such finalists: Wilson (twice), David Henry Hwang, María Irene Fornés, and Anna Deavere Smith. Since 1994, five playwrights of color have won the top prize for drama: Ayad Akhtar, Quiara Alegría Hudes, Lynn Nottage, Nilo Cruz, and Suzan-Lori Parks. In the same period, fourteen have been finalists: Stephen Karam, Kristoffer Diaz, Rajiv Joseph, Lin Manuel Miranda with Quiara Alegría Hudes, David Henry Hwang, Eisa Davis, Quiara Alegría Hudes, Dael Orlandersmith, August Wilson (twice), Suzan-Lori Parks, and Cornelius Eady with Deirdre Murray. This trickle of critical attention widening to a current of validation for diverse voices led to the watershed 2016 Pulitzer Prize going to Lin-Manuel Miranda for *Hamilton*. The hip-hop-infused smash Broadway musical and cultural phenomenon speaks to a demographically changed America, not only remixing the Founding Fathers, but remaking the American musical.

Of equal, if not greater importance than the validation of these writers through major award programs, is the work of leading theaters across the country that have created pathways of development and production. Among them are many whose artistic directors suggested playwrights for this book, including André Bishop, Lincoln Center Theater; Peter Brosius,

Children's Theatre Company; Tisa Chang, Pan Asian Repertory Theatre; Tim Dang, East West Players; Oskar Eustis, The Public Theater; Kamilah Forbes, Hi-Arts; Michael John Garcés, Cornerstone Theater; James Houghton, Signature Theatre; Jamil Khoury, Silk Road Rising; Dipankar Mukherjee, Pangea World Theater; Jim Nicola, the New York Theatre Workshop; Jose Ortoll and Ralph Peña of Ma-Yi Theater; Bill Rausch, Oregon Shakespeare Festival; Randy Reinholz, Native Voices; Rosalba Rolón, Pregones Theater; Abe Rybeck, Theater Offensive; and José Luis Valenzuela of the Los Angeles Theatre Center.

The leading practices of historic theaters of color, several in the aforementioned, cannot be overstated in nurturing and championing diverse playwrights, directors, designers, production staff, and administrators. These theaters have been the primary sites for culturally sensitive production, consistent and ongoing artist development, and a deep commitment to community building. Some have made critical transitions to new artistic leaders that are steeped in the theater's history, like Sade Lythcott and Jonathan McCrory at the National Black Theater, Kinan Valdez at El Teatro Campesino, and Sarah Bellamy at Penumbra Theatre. These artists are bridging earlier cultural movements and activism with the contemporary moment. Others, like Mia Katigbak of the National Asian American Theatre Company have broadened their producing vision to embrace other writers of color, as well as the European and European American canon.

Innovative models of organizing are being led by playwrights such as Keith Josef Adkins co-founder of New Black Fest or Jorge Cortiñas co-founder of Fulcrum Theater. They are determining not just what to produce, but re-thinking how to produce. For example Adkins commissioned *Facing Our Truth,* a festival of 10-minute plays catalyzed by the death of Trayvon Martin; around the country it has created a focal point for organizing about violence against black men. Many theater artists of color, like Jenny Koons and Clinton Lowe of Artist 4 Change NYC, see social activism as intrinsic to their art; they are increasingly taking on hybrid roles as actors/writers/directors/producers/activist organizers. Unprecedented coalitions of theaters, arts organizations, and independent theater artists of color are being built through new national convenings and festivals. The HowlRound commons howlround.com provides critical access to significant national efforts underway like the Latina/o Theatre Encuentro, the

National Asian American Theater ConFest, and the Catalyst Convening of Black Theaters. Leading-edge producing, presenting and organizing models with diverse leadership and programs including the Network of Ensemble Theaters, the Brave New Voices Festival, the Hemi Encuentro, and the Under the Radar Festival are animating theater across borders of genre and geography.

The widening of the theatrical canon has created the possibility of greater opportunities for theater artists of color and the potential for building theater audiences that are reflective of the cities and nation in which the theaters reside. The twenty-first century conversation for artists of color in the theater is no longer about whether there is room for these extraordinary creative voices in the American theater, but how the American theater will change beyond the stage—from diverse artistic leadership, to inclusive boards and staff, equitable partnerships and engagement of community, and new models of making theater.

These monologues are markers on the roadmap of a country where the cultural terrain is radically reshaping. I hope they will lead actors to revelatory moments of performance—and theater makers and audiences to the longer works of extraordinary writers illuminating the way.

Roberta Uno
New York City

Acknowledgements

The Editor wishes to thank the following artistic directors, playwrights, and arts advocates for their suggestions of playwrights to consider and their wonderful enthusiasm for this project: Elissa Adams, André Bishop, Ed Bourgeois, Peter C. Brosius, Lucy Burns, Alison Carey, Emilya Cachapero, Tisa Chang, Rachel Cooper, Tim Dang, Snehal Desai, Julie Felise Dubiner, John Clinton Eisner, Oskar Eustis, Kamilah Forbes, Michael John Garcés, Lydia Garcia, Hanay Geiogamah, Malik Gillani, James Houghton, Marc Bamuthi Joseph, Melanie Joseph, Diane Kaplan, Jamil Khoury, Dipankar Mukherjee, Meena Natarajan, Jim Nicola, Jorge Ortoll, Joan Osato, Ralph Peña, Kathy A. Perkins, Bill Rauch, Randy Reinholz, Betsy Theobald Richards, Rosalba Rolón, Abe Rybeck, Megan Sandberg-Zakian, Robert Schenkkan, Ryan Sueoka, Vicky Holt Takamine, José Luis Valenzuela, Meiyin Wang, Susan Whitmore, and Chay Yew.

Thanks to the following actors for helping with the selection process by doing readings of some of these texts so I could hear how they play: Kristen Adele Calhoun, Cleo Gray, Carvens Lissaint, Richard McDonald, Margaret Odette, and Leta Renée-Alan.

Thanks to the following theater artists and activists who generously provided their perspectives including: Farah Bala, Ty Defoe, Russell G. Jones, Mia Katigbak, Jinn S. Kim, Jenny Koons, Clinton Lowe, Sade Lythcott, Jonathan McCrory, and Rosalba Rolón.

Thanks to Kristen Adele Calhoun for manuscript preparation.

And for their love, patience and support always: Andrew Condron, Chinua Akimaro Thelwell, and Mikiko Akemi Thelwell.

Permissions

after all the terrible things I do

A. Rey Pamatmat

From "Closing Shift" (Scene 3). An independent bookstore in an average-sized, unremarkable Midwestern town. Now.

Linda, late 40s, Filipina, is a typical American immigrant and the owner of Books to the Sky, an independent bookstore. She has recently hired Daniel, a young, aspiring novelist who has just graduated from college. The pair forms an intimate bond when they discover that bullying has played a significant and painful role in both their pasts. But their kinship ends when Linda discovers that Daniel was not a victim of bullying like her dead son but a bully himself.

In this monologue, Linda names Daniel for the coward he is while confronting her own role in her son's tragic end.

LINDA: I KNOW WHAT YOU ARE! We both know what we are! I KILLED MY SON! I KILLED MY SON!!!

When Isaac learned what those words on his locker meant—faggot, queer, homo—he said to me, "They're not bad words, mommy. They're words for boys who want to kiss boys."

And I said, "It doesn't matter. No one should call you that."
And then Isaac said to me, "But I do want to kiss boys, mommy."
And I smacked him.
I smacked him so hard I couldn't send him to school the next day.
I forgot I could be that angry until the night in the store with you.
I told him he should never say that again and certainly never, ever do it.

Isaac grew. He would tell me someone at school ruined his things or hurt him, and instead of telling him everything was alright, I told him he should stop wearing that shirt or walking like that or talking so much and so fast and so gay. And I would make him speak to me with his hands at his sides, so he wouldn't wave them around. And I would make him deepen his voice. And I would tell him to stop being friends with those girls and not to be seen with that boy.

But it didn't stop. And after every horrible incident all I ever said was, "What did you do? Who were you with? What did you say?"

And then he took his own life.

And do you know what the first emotion I felt was? Relief. It wasn't all I felt or even most of it. But it was the first thing. I wouldn't have to raise a gay son. We would never fight about what I wanted for him. He would never leave his family for a man.

And it was actually hard for me, at first, to hate his bullies. To not think that that's what happens to gay people, as though he should have expected this.

Then two years later my husband left me for not being as destroyed as he was. And I left the church—I couldn't go back, I don't know why. And then ten years after I smacked my nine year old son simply because he trusted me, all of that anger faded away, and I looked around, and I was alone. No son. No husband. No family. Just this store. And I have tried never to get that angry again.

But then you told me about that boy who trusted you. Who you betrayed so completely that all he could do was...what Isaac did. You were the person who should have loved him the most, but you couldn't, so how could he love himself? And I knew what I was.

I taught Isaac how little he was worth. All he did was act on what I taught him, taking that first smack to its inevitable conclusion. I killed him.

You aren't who I want you to be, and I want to kill you for it. That night I felt helpless, and my instinct was to hurt you like I hurt my son.

See? I know what I am. So do you. We're cowards.

Aftermath

Jessica Blank and Erik Jensen

Outside of Iraq, 2008.

Basima, an Iraqi refugee and young mother (late 20s–30s) addresses the audience directly as she tells the story of the bombing that decimated her family.

BASIMA: I gave birth in July. Our first child. And when he was two months old, it came time for us to get him vaccinations. (*long beat*) So—we were on the way to the doctor's with the baby. Everyone came in the car, me and my husband and my mother and my son and my sister—because my sister was just seventeen, we couldn't leave her alone in the house, someone, the militias…could come into the house and…(*beat. she can't say it. finally*):…and hurt her.

In the car, we were all just happy with the baby and fussing, would this vaccination go okay, would he cry, would he feel better.

And then, all of a sudden—*ya3ni*, sound, and heat, lots of heat. And, the smell of burnt hair and flesh. And pain. The car shook, hard, and right away I lost my sight.

I don't know how I got out of the car. I couldn't see. The thing I could hear most was the sound of my husband's voice. I just followed the sound back to him.

He wanted to get out of the car but his legs were fused to the seat. I tried to get him out, but he was heavy, I couldn't I couldn't. I felt the fire start to eat at my hands. I tried to get him out, I tried, but *I couldn't*. (*beat*) So I left. I called for whoever could help me. I was yelling at the top of my lungs. But there wasn't any person, there wasn't anybody. It was as if the world had ended.

And then another explosion, and screaming and yelling. And then my husband's voice disappears.

I hear bullets from every direction. And I'm barefoot, and I can't see and I don't know what to do so I just sit down. There's nobody there. Nobody nobody. It is as if Baghdad has been emptied of people.

Of course, you know, this accident was on Al Jazeera. They showed me like—my blouse was open. My clothes were burned off. And I'm asking, what happened, where's my husband, my son, my mother, my sister. One Muslim guy, do you know what he says to me? He says (*clearly mocking*) "They went to Allah."

From 10:30 till 12:30 I was in the street. After two hours I heard the blades of a helicopter. Americans came, they were speaking English. They were checking out what the explosion was. It was a long time till they came to me. I was secondary. But whatever I can say about the accident wouldn't be enough. (*to translator*) Translate this, okay, so that they can...(*she needs a break*).

Another Part of the House

Migdalia Cruz

Act 2, two months after Act 1, at the end of a long afternoon in Bernarda Alba's bedroom, in a modest farmhouse in Santa Clara, in the province of Las Villas, Cuba, 1895.

In this re-imagining of Garcia-Lorca's *La Casa de Bernarda Alba*, Bernarda, 60, the pious matriarch of the Alba family, has just been told by Poncia, the family maid, that her daughters fear her more than love her. She blames her mother's wildness, and her dead husband, Antonio's licentiousness for the sexual inappropriateness and ungodliness of their daughters.

Here, she tells his portrait what she really thinks of him in a rare, honest moment alone.

BERNARDA: I have to do something about my mother. She's pulling my house down into the grave with her. I won't have it. Not again. (*Bernada crosses to the portrait of her recently dead husband, Don Antonio and speaks to it.*) I—never loved you, Antonio. That was my secret. But you knew it. I endured every child—every child a female. A torture. Because I knew what I had to teach them and give them so that they could turn out better than I ever could. A boy would have been so much easier. You can ignore them. But girls have to be trained to keep their legs together. Without the training they become whores or servants or worse—poor. So poor that they can't stop begging for everything they get. Only begging keeps those kinds of girls alive. No one in this family will ever beg. And that's my doing, husband. Mine! Where were you in this? Where were you ever? I wish I could cry for your dead soul, but I can't Antonio. For the first time in many years, I can finally hear myself speak. Because your desire isn't drowning me, filling every pore in my skin with wetness. Being alone now is like a desert, and I feed on that sand that keeps you out of me. Stay away, Antonio. I'll wear black forever if you'll just stay away—from me and from my daughters. Everything you taught them could kill them. I have to undo you from us all. (*Bernarda takes down Don Antonio's portrait and exits with it under her arm.*) Maybe I'll bury you.

Becoming Cuba

Melinda Lopez

Act 1, scene 2. A pharmacy in Havana, Cuba, 1898.

Hatuey's Wife is ageless and the color of rebellion.

Hatuey was the great Taino warrior who led the first resistance against the Spanish Conquistadors in the Caribbean. We know his wife was also a great leader, but we don't know very much else about her. In the play *Becoming Cuba*, Hatuey's Wife makes an unscheduled appearance. She talks directly to the audience, and although characters onstage feel her, they don't know she's there. She is part of the spirit world that walks the island of Cuba—those people lost in the many battles to conquer and re-conquer the land.

HATUEY'S WIFE: (*She is dressed in traditional Taino garb, and speaks like a warrior queen, by way of Union City.*)

To understand me, you have to remember me.

Let me rest in a corner of your mind, as I was, dressed in leather and flowers, a Taino queen. A warrior. A mother.

One of The First Nation.

Everyone says that I was enamored of the men who landed that day. That the lust of Hatuey's Wife was insatiable. That I thought the men with yellow hair and silver skin were gods.

Seriously? Have you white people looked at yourselves? Have you been to a beach lately? White people are so ugly. For real! Like they're radioactive.

All skin peeling off and hair plastered to their faces by the sweat. Why do you sweat so much? Skinny, anemic looking, all pasty and pale.

Gods? What kind of god gets a sunburn?

No, I wasn't thinking they were beautiful. I knew they were men. I'm not stupid. Deformed men, under all the armor. I thought they must be hideous to cover themselves like that. We have a man like that, and we never let him out of the cave where he lives. The sight of his body is offensive. I thought the white men were like him. Maybe they had been cast off from their land of beautiful brown people—too many of them to keep tied up, so the queen sent them away in this spaceship, over the ocean.

I felt sorry for them. Hatuey's Wife. Soft in the heart and in the head.

I invited them to dinner. Cooked up a big vat of frijoles. 200 partridges on a spit. Wild boar. Yuca and maduros. Chile and lime juice. They came, they ate. And then they killed us. Yeah. I know. For real. While it was happening, I thought, this is the worst party ever.

Butterfly

Jeremy Tiang

A dim sum restaurant in London. The present.

Mui Foong is in her thirties and originally from Hong Kong. She has renamed herself Butterfly, after the Puccini opera. She was married to a British man but is now divorced, and struggling to meet men while working as a waitress in a dim sum restaurant. It must be said that Butterfly doesn't entirely understand the world around her, but is doing her very best to make sense of it. Although she has lived in London for more than ten years, her English is still imperfect. When her boss at the restaurant asks her to emcee an event, she is naturally thrilled to take her moment in the limelight, which she also sees as an opportunity to practice her speaking skills. She then gets somewhat carried away, and ends up telling the audience more about her love life than is strictly appropriate.

BUTTERFLY (MUI FOONG): This is fun, talking to you like this. Helps me practice my English. You don't mind, do you? At home I have only my cat to talk to, and he doesn't correct my grammar. Very selfish, cats. My English teacher Bradley told me I didn't need to worry, my English is "awesome." He's from San Francisco. I like that word, "awesome." Like Cantonese. Aw sum.

He's very handsome, Bradley. He always smells so nice. Good teeth and that kind of—you say California tan? He has California tan.

When my husband left me, all my friends said, What do you expect, marrying a gwailo. Ah, "gwailo"—it means "devil person." What we call white people.

Sorry, that's not very nice, but when you start a fake war about opium and then colonize our country for one hundred years, you must expect a certain amount of lingering resentment.

He left me for a Taiwanese woman. It won't last. Do you know what the Taiwanese word for buffet is? "Chi dao bao." That means eat until full. Eat until full! In Hong Kong, full is only the beginning. She'll starve him to death.

For a Cantonese person, hungry is the worst thing to be. We sacrifice food to our ancestors so they won't have to starve. If I don't hurry up and have kids soon, there'll be no altar full of roast duck for me. My spirit will have to hang out at the dumpsters behind KFC.

In Hong Kong, we call buffet "zi zo caan." Help-yourself meal. Everything is help yourself, as much as you like. Of course, he helped himself and helped himself, and then he left me.

My mother said, Mui Foong, I told you not to marry a gwailo, that story never has a happy ending—look at Pocahontas. I said, Ma, I'm not bitter, maybe I'll be happier without him in my life, maybe he'll be better off with that Taiwanese bitch. Maybe it's fate. She said, Mui Foong, we're Cantonese, we don't believe in fate, we believe in punishment. I said, Ma, you're thinking of the Catholics.

I'm not Catholic, by the way. Methodist. We're even stricter. Not even wine at communion. Kool-Aid in little plastic cups. I like to imagine Jesus turning water into Kool-Aid.

In the end I asked myself, what would Jesus do? So I looked at my horoscope—because Jesus was born on December twenty-fifth, which makes him a Capricorn, just like me. I didn't like the one in the Times—something about being realistic—but the one in Time Out said to take a chance on someone close to me. And so I asked Bradley out on a date. I didn't tell my mother. Still I heard her voice, in my head, What, Mui Foong, another gwailo? Why can't you learn? So I answered back—in my head—Ma, this one is different, he has nice teeth. He smells good. (My ex-husband always smelt like feet.)

Bradley said he wanted to go to the ballet. I thought, Okay, interesting choice. So he has culture. We went to a nice bar first. He ordered rosé, which matched his shirt, and then I told him about my ex-husband, and he told me about his ex-boyfriend.

And I had to say, Sorry, maybe my English is not very good, but when you say "boyfriend", do you mean a friend who happens to be a boy, or—

When I told my friends about this later, they said, Duh, he took you to the ballet. How do people know these things? These clues. Life is hard enough without having to guess.

Café Vida

Lisa Loomer

Act 1, Scene 1. A Los Angeles jail. Now.

Chabela, 20s, Mexican American, is getting out of jail right now. In this monologue, she talks about being a "fuck-it-fat", meth addicted gang banger…about to go on the first job interview of her life. We follow her on the bus where she's accompanied by the DJ who lives in her head singing mariachi, oldies, and rap…all the way to downtown.

In this monologue, she's talking to the audience…Us.

CHABELA: Oye. Sabes que? Got a interview this morning with Father Tim, downtown. Said come see him when I got out of prison—(*realizes she's the only one talking to the audience now*) Oh! Name's Chabela, short for Isabel, which I don't like cause it sounds too fuckin' girly, but my homies call me Flaca which means "Skinny", 'cause I'm fat. (*to a woman in the audience*) You got a problem with that? (*laughs*) No, I'm not curvy, I'm not chunky, I'm not plus size, bootylicious, I'm not, "Hey, baby, I like me some of that"… I'm fat! Not gringa girl fat, like "Oh, I just ate so much I went up to a size two!" I'm "fuck-it" fat. I'm "Get outta my way, I'm goin' back for thirds" fat. And I don't have no eating disorder or no slow ass metabolism—I just like to <u>eat</u>. (*to another woman in audience*) That's right, esa, Big Mac, fries and a shake, like-to-eat. Half a pepperoni pizza with extra cheese like-to-eat. Coldstone cookie dough with fudge and Reese's, and gimme the Big Cup. So coupla years ago, when I heard they was hiring for Homeboy's <u>bakery</u>…I said, "Fuck yeah!" (*beat*) Unfortunately, at the time I was still doing meth, which didn't do shit to kill my appetite by the way, but it did kinda kill my ability to like...show up on time? Well, show up at all, to tell you la verdad. But when I got out this time and heard about this other job? Man, I felt like I died and gone to heaven dos veces! Cause <u>this</u> job is at—sound of angels please... Un <u>café</u>! (*She notices someone in the first row staring and mad dogs the lady*) Whatchu lookin' at? (*pats her big belly*) You don't use protection? Maybe you don't do it with tacos—(*pats her thighs*) Or Ben Y Jerry's... But maybe you like a coupla of nice cold forties all to yourself, que no? Nice fat layer 'tween you and Out There? Nice layer of bubble wrap 'tween you and Them? (*laughs*) Gotta have protection, right? Can't have too much of <u>that</u>...(*She pulls on a big t-shirt and baggy pants.*) Now where's my bag at? (*yells to wings*) I got a interview, pendejo! (*to audience*) Orale. Let's go. (*Sound of a bus, as the bus stop is projected.*) Okay, it's fifteen minutes to downtown if you steal a Lex or even a Honda...But I can't do that no more...So it's two hours on the bus. (*She holds on to an imaginary strap*) Luckily, I always got a song in my head. (*to man in audience*) Man, like you don't? Like you're on the bus... And in your head you got this song... (*She sings a few lines of "Guadalajara" the mariachi tune, full throttle.*) Okay—not that song. Maybe... (*She sings a few lines of a rap song, then stops abruptly.*) Okay, maybe an oldie. Something romantic. (*She sings a few lines of, "Thin Line Between Love and Hate." Then—*) Okay. So you're on the bus and you realize—hey, that song's been in my head since I got on in South Gate and now I'm halfway to downtown! Whatever. Nobody knows you're a bubble wrapped chola with a DJ in your head. They think you just another fat chick on your way to work. (*beat. scared to death now*) Nobody knows you never had a job in your whole fuckin' life.

Café Vida

Lisa Loomer

Act 2, Scene 2. A meeting of Criminals and Gang Members Anonymous in Los Angeles. Now.

Chabela, 20s, Mexican American, is working at Café Vida, a restaurant/ training program which rehabilitates gang members. The play follows her struggle to leave la vida loca and make a new life. But this monologue comes at a point in the play when Chabela has fucked up bad and gotten into a fight with a co-worker. As part of her program, she's gotta go to this meeting... And worse, she's gotta "share."

In this monologue she's addressing a room full of homies, fellow gang bangers.

CHABELA: Hi, my name is Chabela and I am a recovering gang member. (*nervous*) Uhm, I been coming to this meeting for about two weeks now, and this is my first time sharing... Guess my knees are kinda shaking... (*jokes*) Specially the one that's still got the bullet... Anyways... I'm supposed to talk about what it was like, what changed, and what it's like now. So, like my tia used to say, here goes nothin'. (*clears her throat*) I started hanging out with the gang when I was at Hollenbeck. (*to an audience member*) That's Middle School. I'd walk through the front door right to the back. I'd go to my neighborhood, kick back, play music, drink, dance... I started getting high when I was about eleven... Rock cocaine, mostly, they used to sell in front of my house. When I was little I used to get molested by my uncle, and my aunt didn't believe me... So I just started saying, "Fuck it" and getting high. I was staying over at my girlfriend's a lot and she was in a gang, and I was like, "Okay! How do I get in?" My girlfriend, she had to throw some dice and whatever number came up, that's how many homies she had to sleep with—(*laughs*) And I wasn't about to do that... So I went to her boys and said, "Who do I got to fight?" I had a choice between six girls for two minutes or one guy for a minute and a half, so I fought this guy Dreamer and got jumped in. After that, whenever something would happen to me, I'd just tell my homeboys and they'd take care of it. Like when I was fifteen I got raped by three border brothers and the only ones that helped me was my homies. So I kept on banging and I was like that all my life. My dream when I was younger was to be in prison, I actually wanted to get there—Juvy, the whole thing! The jail would call up my aunt and she'd say, "Keep her, I don't know what to do with her." (*beat; matter of fact*)

I guess the worst thing I ever did was when this girl Tiny that was one of our enemies set up my homeboy, and we went driving around and found her and put her in the car, and I was on meth at the time, and I was like banging her head on the dashboard and then I used my boot and nearly stomped her to death. She was hanging half out the car, and we passed two cop cars and they didn't do a thing! I took this like, broke off stick from a broom, and stuck her between the legs... And then we just threw her out the car... (*bursts into tears*) And I will regret that my whole life. (*beat; cold*) But I didn't stop banging. (*long beat*) I had my daughter when I was seventeen in Sybil Brand. I just wanted to have a kid before I died, you know? When I was pregnant, I was getting high every day, and she came out positive for alcohol and cocaine. And she was crying 'cause she was kicking the drugs. She was so little, she fit in a shoe box. I call her my miracle baby. (*beat; fighting tears*) With my son... He came out dirty too... And that's what made me want to change. (*beat*) But a few weeks ago, I got in a fight. Look–I'm not used to working with women, okay? When I was in the gang, some of the girls would disrespect themselves and go with vatos from other neighborhoods, so I was always working by myself or with the homeboys– (*emotional*) And I–I don't trust women, okay?! (*beat*) So now I'm on step two in this program, 'bout came to believe in a Higher Power? Mostly, I'm like, "Okay, lemme just borrow Father T's High Power." But Gaby gave me this calendar with a picture of the Virgen de Guadalupe? And last night I'm counting the days till I stop being suspended... And I look at the Virgen—and she got that green cape with all the stars? And for the first time, I notice... Shit! It's shooting flames! Man, she got these—flames!—just shooting out from all over her! And I mean, damn! Who's gonna mess with <u>that</u>? So now I'm like, "Hey, if it's not too much trouble, I like to get me some of <u>that</u> Higher Power..." (*beat*) And guess we'll see what she says. Anyways... Thanks.

Calling Aphrodite

Velina Hasu Houston

Act 2. Scene 14. A New York hospital clinic's garden, 1955.

Keiko Kimura (18–28) is a Hiroshima bomb victim who reluctantly goes to New York as part of The Hiroshima Maidens Project in order to support her eager sister, Shizuko (16–26). The play explores Keiko's journey from pre-war to its aftermath. In the monologue, Keiko shuns involvement in the project because her sister, the first to be operated on, died from an anesthesia overdose. Keiko remains outside of the meeting where Dr. Everett, the lead U.S. physician, convenes with several Japanese bomb victims. Reverend Matsubayashi, a project advocate who has traveled with the bomb victims from Hiroshima, has implored Keiko to participate, but given what she has lost in form and function at the hands of an American bomb along with the death of her parents and sister, she is reluctant to so readily play a part in the project. She tries to make the reverend understand why she cannot without difficulty have faith in her former enemy.

KEIKO: The Hiroshima Maidens Project already has a bad name. The Japanese don't trust it because it's a "gift" from the same people who practiced nuclear holocaust on human beings for the first time in history. The Americans don't like it because they don't understand why American money is being spent on Japanese girls to "make us look pretty." Maybe we know that they're not trying to make us look pretty, that they're trying to fix our hands and feet, reasonable form and function, but nobody else knows that. Look at how sure you are about my sister's death. Were you there in the operating room with all of those doctors? Men of God? What does that mean, to be "men of God"? Does that mean they are infallible? Does that mean they are incapable of hatred or revenge? A gift? Pardon me, but it is not a gift to me. I questioned it, but, no, good Japanese women bow and acquiesce. We don't question anything. We accept whomever our fathers choose for us to marry. We accept whatever bombs an American president wants to test on us. I'm tired of politely smiling and bowing: yield, defer, resign yourself. The Japanese mantra is killing me. My country may survive, but what about my spirit? Who cares what the Americans think of us? All they say is that our green tea's flavorless and our coffee isn't good enough. Don't you know they're doing this project just because they feel guilty for dropping atomic bombs on children? Listen to you. You're so in love with America. Just like my sister. We're dying of radiation sickness. What difference is all of this really going to make? Who's to blame? President Truman? Oppenheimer? Tojo? Or that very popular choice: fate? I'll tell you: nobody. It can't be helped. Why all these operations to make us look as if the bomb never fell? It did. It's done. We pick up the pieces and move on. You say it will make us better men. What about the women? Maybe men make war, but women suffer, too. (*pause*)

You don't know what it's like to get up in the morning and realize the person you loved most is gone. Forever. I'll never be able to look at her, listen to her silly dreams, or even argue with her again.

Contigo

Paola Lázaro-Muñoz

Scene 2. A laundromat in New York City, nowadays.

Dena is a strong and tough young woman in her mid to late 20s. At this moment Dena is addressing Tigo. Tigo is a young Puerto Rican man in his mid 20s. Straight from the island he moved to NYC a couple of years ago with his lifelong best friends Lolipop and Rafa. Tigo is miserable and sleeps about 20 hours a day. Rafa is Dena's longtime boyfriend. Rafa is a heavy duty, loving, but rather obsessive and intense young man in his late 20s. We don't know this yet in the story, but Dena has been taken advantage of sexually by Rafa (her boyfriend) and since then she has not been the same. Dena and Tigo had a close encounter in a bathroom last night and although nothing physical happened between them, the sexual tension and proximity of their faces was enough to keep you fantasizing about it. Now the two of them are discussing last night's events in the bathroom. Tigo is denying their connection and Dena explodes.

DENA: Fuck, Fuck my life in half! Fuck! (*She looks at him*) Shit. Forget it. Forget it. I can't—Oh fuck me! Fuck me! Shit like this always happens to me!

Before I come when I'm masturbating I get all these thoughts fucking exploding in my head and I try to think about other men—but I can't come, I can't come, I can't and the rubbing's in vain and that shit hurts and then your name, your name pops up and explodes and I come and I shake—and I have to hold the frame of my bed cause I'm imagining you fucking me so hard that I have to hold myself—I have to hold some shit so I don't melt—float the fuck away—smoking Marlboro Reds til four thirty in the morning in my room fucking thinkin bout you. And I try not to do it—but—(*His mouth is open, frozen.*) What am I saying? Fuck! What am I saying? What am I doing to myself?

Shit! Forget it! Forget everything I just said. My life is great. My life is great. My life is fuckin great. Control our thoughts—that's that shit that the Buddha says—I gotta practice that shit—my life is great. (*His mouth is still open. She starts to walk out.*) Fuck. It's not. It's not. I'm fucking shit up. I'm fucking shit up. I'm fucking some shit. I'm fucking everything up. (She turns back.) You know, I can't sleep lately—I don't know how to put myself to sleep. Rafa always falls asleep first. And I can't sleep.

And I blame him for being able to sleep and for not staying up with me. For not enduring shit with me and I just lay in bed. I smoke a cigarette thinkin that's all I need to be able to sleep.

I smoke it and it ain't enough. So I smoke a bowl, thinkin it'll be enough, but it ain't enough. I masturbate next to him, I come, and it ain't enough. And I know he knows. And pretends not to.

Fuck! And now I've gone and said all this shit. That always happens to me—I say too much shit and then I can't go back to erase it. (*She remembers*) And fuck! I even mentioned the masturbating thing!

The Convert

Danai Gurira

Act 3 Scene 3. The late 1890s. The Lounge of Chilford Ndhlovu's home, in the Boomtown of Salisbury (Present day Harare, Zimbabwe).

"The room is modestly furnished, with great Victorian influence, though a very impoverished version." Evening. Jekesai-Ester, a Zimbabwean girl in her late teens with "an unavoidable keenness and resolve in her eye" enters "wrapped in a large zambia (African scarf)." Jekesai has converted to Catholicism to escape an arranged marriage and she finds herself torn between the bloody cultural revolution of her people and her newfound religious devotion.

In this monologue, she reveals that she murdered the white couple that have held her in their employ as a way of avenging her cousin's death. She confesses to her spiritual father, Chilford and asks for his absolution.

JEKESAI: I am confessing—everything. I have to tell you something now, Master. The time is not long. I…(*Beat*) they killed him like a chicken Master. A chicken. (*Beat*) He kept, he kept looking at me—I know what it was he was thinking. He was thinking I have this good English and this bible learning why I couldn't stop them like I was saying I could. Why I couldn't save him this time. Just this one time. And I couldn't. I couldn't do one thing. I just was standing there with my bible like a fool, like a dofo. So I had to… I had to, …I…(*Beat*) They were sleeping, Master and Mistress Coltern, when she see me, I am thinking she thought I was just coming to be warning them of something. I am a good one. That is what they would always be telling me—You are one of the good ones Ester.

I like being good Master. But I couldn't, I couldn't *manage.* (*Beat*) Master, you have never told me about you your father but I want to tell you about mine. My father was a good, good man. And today, today I meet him. And he was angry with me. He told me to shed blood for my own. The whites don't do what their book it is saying. I thought they would be like Jesus, show his love, love their enemy, I thought—(*Beat*) I wanted to not care and spill their blood like they were not caring and spilling mine. They killed him like a chicken Master. A *chicken.* (*Beat*) She open her eyes, Mrs. Coltern, her eyes they were looking at me like she know me—but she did not know me today. Amai always called me the best with the chickens, I could do it one time, I knew how to cut quick, how to lift the knife just like so and drop it heavy. I just lift the knife like I do with the chicken and drop it through Mrs. Coltern she her neck. I think if I drop it somewhere else she would have been screaming but I was cutting the neck so she just open her mouth and it look like the sound it want to come but it can't. Her eyes they looking at me like she can't believe. Him he not even wake up, I leave him like that—to sleep, I just put it the knife in his breast many, many time. I see it, the blood, somehow it make me to feel better. I know their kind bleed like my cousin he bleed; their blood it was looking like his, same color, it come out same. I was thinking, maybe it a difference but no, we have same under this (*tugging at the skin on her arm, her zambia drops to the ground, revealing her blood drenched arms and dress*) just the same. (*Dawn begins to break*) Master, can you be absolving me?

Doin' Time: Through the Visiting Glass

Ashley Lucas

Arizona, sometime in the first decade of the twenty-first century.

Doin' Time is a one-act play comprised of monologues of thirteen differ-ent characters, usually all performed by a single actor. Each character in the play has a loved one in prison, and the combined effect of all the characters' voices provides a small window into the diversity and com-plexity of the lives of the millions of people in the United States whose families and communities are interrupted by prison walls and razor wire.

Lola is a teenage Chicana. This is the only time we meet her in the play.

LOLA: My brother's an artist. He draws and paints, but mostly he does graffiti. Now he's doin seven years—for graffiti. Can you imagine? Seven years of your life for a crime where nobody got hurt. Who's it helpin for him to be in prison? The guy whose wall he wrote on? Shit. It woulda helped that guy more if the court gave my brother community service and made him clean up the pinche wall.

I think mostly they locked him up because he's a smart ass. We saw a mural once when we was kids that said "God Is Mexican," and Danny, my brother, loved that shit. When we got back to Phoenix, he started writing it on walls all over the place. God is a Chicana. Dios es un mojado. God comes from the barrio. God hangs out at Tito's. He went on like that for years. Got really good, too. He didn't just paint the words. He made them beautiful.

We were raised Catholic, but my mother was real non-traditional. She took us to church every Sunday, and we prayed like everybody else, but during the rest of the week Amá talked to God like he was her compadre or somethin. She talked to Him like he was right there washing the dishes and doin the laundry with her. She got mad at God, too. Told him when he was bein stupid, and then she'd apologize to God later when she wasn't mad no more. She'd say, "Perdóname, Diosito. I'm sorry, but I was angry with you this morning for sending rain on the day of Lolita's first communion, pero I realize now that you send the bad weather so that the wind would blow Doña Violeta's ugly dress over her head on the steps of the church to punish her for being una vieja chismosa. Now that your plan has been revealed to me, I apologize for yelling at you and for stealing five extra communion wafers porque tenía hambre durante la misa. Ya no quiero hablar más de eso."

Anyways we grew up having an unusual relationship with God because of my mother, and then a bunch of my brother's friends got arrested, and if Danny'd been with them that night, he woulda got picked up, too. That really freaked him out, and he started goin to all the places where he used to paint "God dances cumbias" and "God is an undocumented immigrant," and he started writing all his friends' names instead. Aldo Gutiérrez is in prison. Israel Cienfuegos is in prison. Freddie Ramírez is in prison. The day the cops caught him he was writing, "David Archuleta is in prison. God is with him. God is a prisoner."

Danny tried to run when he saw the cops, but they caught him. Three of them beat him until them gave him a concussion and broke his right hand so that he don't write so good no more. Amá stopped talking to God for a week, and now Danny writes us letters in real shaky handwriting. At the bottom underneath his signature he always writes, "God is a prisoner."

Fati's Last Dance

France-Luce Benson

Act 1. Scene 1. A brownstone in Brooklyn, NY. The home of Gislene LaBelle, in the living room, early evening. The present.

Fatima La Belle is a first generation Haitian-American woman in her late 20s.

The eldest daughter of two professional dance icons, Fatima has the talent to continue her family's legacy. But after her father's untimely death, and her mother's unrelenting criticism, she gives up dancing completely. Depressed, Fatima's life revolves around watching television and binging on junk food. Then, her mother announces that Fatima's father will be posthumously honored with a prestigious award. The celebration at Carnegie Hall will include a tribute dance, and a documentary produced by Spike Lee. But when her mother asks Fatima's sister, Roni, to perform, Fatima is outraged. Fatima is determined to perform the tribute herself. Haunted by mysterious messages from her father's ghost, and desperate to prove herself, Fatima falls prey to a popular infomercial Guru. The disastrous effects serve as the catalyst for the family to confront their grief, and heal old wounds. In this scene, Fatima's mother has just informed her that she is choosing Roni to perform the tribute; and suggests that Fatima is jealous of her sister's success. Fatima fires back at her mother.

FATIMA: Does she really think I'm that shallow? I have a Bachelors degree in Political Science. I was the President of Amnesty International in High School. I spent half a year with Volunteers for Humanity, planting trees in the Amazon Rainforest. I don't care how pretty Roni is, she's evil. And the two of them together are like, like Elvira, and, Evilene—sucking at my blood. I swear, if Roni showed up here tomorrow, I would ease my big butt down the road, right back to Brazil. As much as I hated working for Volunteers for Humanity—the heat, the rain, the bugs—at least they treated me like I meant something. Regardless of what I looked like. Hell, them aborigines thought I was a fox. Especially (*She makes a clicking, gutteral sound*). That was his name. (*Makes the sound*) used to serenade me in the mornings with his Ilú drum. It reminded me of when Daddy used to warm up in the mornings. The studio was right under my bedroom. I used to put my ear to the floor just to hear the clickity-clack of his tap shoes. (*Makes the sound*) wasn't much of a dancer, but man could he play them drums. He wanted to marry me. And I was so messed up that I actually considered it. But I eventually came to my senses. I mean, what was I going to do? Spend the rest of my life hiding behind people who were even uglier than—I didn't mean that. Did I just say that? He wasn't ugly. None of them were. They were beautiful, gentle souls. And that's not why I left. I left because Ma needed me. She needed me, and I came. Like I always do. But ask Ma who really cares, and it's Roni this, and Roni that, and—Let me tell you something about Roni. She's selfish, she's loud, she's ignorant, and she can't dance to save her life. She never could. Still, all I ever hear is, "Oh my god, your sister is Ronielle LaBelle? From America's Next Top Model Cycle 26?" Bitch ain't even win. Soon as she opened her big mouth? Kicked her ratchet behind off in the third week. But she bounced right back up on her perfect little booty. She went on to "Surreal Pseudo-Celebrity Rap Challenge." After that she did "Celebrity Apprentice", then "Dancing With the Stars", and she's spent the past two years starring on "Real Wives of the NFL." And she's not even married! She is LA's reigning reality show queen. And I'm stuck here plucking Evilene's eyebrows.

Fetch Clay, Make Man

Will Power

Act 2. Scene 3. A small, hastily built dressing room, moments before the heavyweight championship rematch. Lewiston, Maine, 1965.

Sonji Clay, the strong willed and loving wife of boxing champion Muhammad Ali, has been struggling with her husband to retain her identity and right to public expression as an African American woman in the complex, turbulent terrain of the 1960s. The bond between her and the young fighter is genuine, however Ali's total allegiance to his religion (The Nation of Islam) has been pushing them further and further apart. Ali lashes out against Sonji for not donning the proper Muslim attire in public. Later Ali discovers a secret that emerges from Sonji's past, and instead of enacting a submissive and apologetic position, Sonji erupts and strongly expresses her right to have a complete and complex expression of their union. In this final showdown between them, Sonji's need for a unification of the past and present explosively collides with Ali's accusations that "with your lyin', wicked ways, what you doin' Sonji is bringing us down."

SONJI CLAY: So, if I would've just put on the Muslim's dress and kept my mouth shut, then everything woulda been alright? Cassius baby, I'm so much more than that. There are so many parts of me that I want to share with you. And I can't go back, I can't pretend to be just a part of me no more. I gotta bring the parts of my life together baby. And I can do it, I can be smart and sexy, and a good wife, and a good mother, and I can do it under one roof. But you say we can't even buy a house 'cause in five years the Mothership's gonna come down and take people away.

Well what about your honorable prophet? Elijah Muhammad has a, have you seen the size of his house? Oh so what they ain't gonn' take Elijah? Why does he get to have a house and we don't? Who are you Cassius Clay? Because if you really are Muhammad Ali, then you would live what you believe, and not do one thing for them, and another when you're with me, like God can't see what you doin'…(*Pause*). Alright… so you want me to leave? (*SONJI leaves the dressing room, passing RASHID on the way out*). He's all yours.

Firebird Tattoo

Ty Defoe

Act 2. Scene 10. Lac Du Flambeau, Reservation. Northern Wisconsin.

Sky, Native American (Anishinabe Tribe) girl who is on the brink of womanhood. Sky comes back to the reservation after being in the city for a while. She puts tradition in question by revealing her tattoos and skin at ceremony. She creates a new ritual and names herself.

SKY: You know what Ma. Forget it. All of this… This isn't for me. This is not traditional. All of this is just to make me stay with you. I know about Raven. I found out. Why wouldn't you just tell me. You say he lied to you, that Phillip lied to you. You know what you lied to me. I lied to you. Yes, I left to go to the city because I had to. I had to find me. Find out who I am. I need to fly and I am soaring. I can't attach myself here anymore. This isn't me. This reservation. This poverty as my culture. (*Sky walks over to the fire and rips open her shirt and reveals her tattoos. The moon turns black. A crack of thunder, singers in the distance with whispers, war cries, and shouts. MA spills sacred strawberry juice everywhere. PHILLIP, D, and WINDIGO watch.*)

There is a time when an *Anishinabe* girl receives a new name. She has a dream for the future, a vision. A symbol. *Ode'imin,* the heart berry. It is red and white in color.

It is the only fruit with the seeds that grow on the outside. On the inside the white bitter color represents the physical growth of adolescence, the struggles, and the forgiveness. It is searching for a place in this life. The red symbolizes blood. The maturing into womanhood, those unfamiliar feelings of fearlessness. I'm going up there!

(*Sky holds her arms up to soar.*)

I forgive. I forgive. I forgive. I forgive. My new name is: Fire Bird. *Ishkoday Binayshii, Ishkoday Binayshii. Ishkoday Binayshii.*

(*Everyone faces the four directions as and repeats in unison like a new ritual. SKY soars up to the smoke and flames.*)

The Frybread Queen

Carolyn Dunn

Top of Act 5. On the Navajo Reservation near Page, Arizona. Time is early morning, 4:30 a.m. A thunderstorm approaches.

Lily Savannah Burns in 17, a full-blood Navajo, dressed in all black with thick, heavy eyeliner. She addresses the audience.

There are four monologues in the play—the Frybread Monologues—in which each of the four characters breaks the fourth wall to plead her case with the audience as to whose frybread recipe is the best. Lily's father has just committed suicide and this monologue takes place the morning after her father's funeral. Lily has been out all night, partying with friends, and is a little wasted. She has learned things about her father's past that have shocked her and now she is an orphan. Her aunt, stepmother, and grandmother are fighting over custody of her. Going with her aunt and stepmother would represent leaving her grandmother's home on the reservation, the only home she has ever known, to faraway Los Angeles. This monologue represents the sharp wit of a self-assured, bitter, and angry young woman—anger at her father's suicide, anger at the stepmother who abandoned her, anger at the adored aunt who has betrayed her—a young Navajo woman coming into her own power, at the cusp of great change.

LILY: How to make frybread, by Lily Santiago Burns. (*Deep breath*) Our history teacher told us that frybread is a fabricated identifier. He said that it's not real Indian food, that it was made to clog Indians' arteries and give us diabetes. And heart disease. White flour fried in lard. A heart attack waiting to happen. All we're doing is frying up common flour in lard and calling it traditional. What the hell is that? What's traditional anyway? Hey, let's be Indians and dress up in beads and buckskin and dance around calling for rain. Oh… I know, give me a leather halter top and a buckskin mini-skirt and I'll run through the woods being chased by falling leaves and singing about the colors of the wind with my eighteen-inch waist and big childbearing hips waiting for some big blond European dude named Colin or…John…to come by and sweet talk me with that cockney of his…and then give me smallpox and bury me in that place he calls home…but I'll survive that and fry some white flour in dough and call it a day. (*Beat*) At least we could get some whole wheat flour, or something. Maybe use olive oil. Or sesame oil, or even sunflower. You know, change the story up a bit. (*Lights fade*).

The Gospel of Lovingkindness

Marcus Gardley

Scene 7. Present Day, Chicago, IL.

Mary Black, middle-aged, African American. Character speaks to anyone who will listen.

The Gospel of Loving Kindness is a play that examines the role of grief, hope and activism in the aftermath of a homicide in the South Side of Chicago. The 90-minute drama details the journey of two mothers, one who is the parent of the slain and the other, the mother of the assailant. What dream for the future can be realized when they come together in the end, or does the future look as bleak as the number of deaths?

In this monologue, Martha is dressed in a postal uniform. She sits and rubs her toes, and talks to us as if we are Mary.

MARTHA: Don't say nothin', Mary. I can already tell by that grin crawling out your lips that you had the time of your life and I'm happy for you but I'm so jealous I could eat my face so don't say a thing. 'Sides, I got work to do. I can't be sittin around all day listenin to you brag about the greatest day of your life when I have mail to mail, stamps to stamp, addresses to readdress. Christmas is days away, people are expecting their cards and since we work for the US Post, we Santa's real helpers, which means we got to save Christmas so….so… (*Time*) So, say something, girl!!! Your boy sung at the White House!!! And y'all is from the South Side of Chicago! How can you stay quiet?! Chile, if it was me I'd wake the whole neighborhood. I'd make T-shirts. I'd get a tattoo on my thigh! Your boy sung at the White House and y'alls is blacks. Ain't even mixed. How can you be quiet? Speak and give me the details and don't leave nothin out not even the pauses. Did you touch him? Obama. Did you smell his neck when you hugged him? He smell like Cocoa Butter don't he? Did you touch his hand? Did you shake it? Did he kiss you on the cheek? Ooo chick, tell me he kissed you on the cheek. I would kill over. I would die with my legs in the air if that fine ass niggah kissed me on my neck—I mean cheek. What you wear? Tell me you didn't wear that seersucker suit you got from Penny's. That suit is a mess and a misdemeanor, I know you didn't wear that, tell me you didn't wear that, Lord, I don't even want to know. Your boy sung Christmas carols at the White House for the black president of these United States. Do you know what this means? You matter now, girl. You've done good; he's got a chance. Wait a minute. Are you smiling? Are you beaming, Mary Black? I been knowing you twenty-two years and I ain't never seen a smile crawl out of your mouth not a once. Well, shit! I likes it. It sets off the diamonds in your eyes. You look like God just put His finishing touches on you, girl. You beaming like a Christmas tree.

Guapa

Caridad Svich

Act 1. Scene 3. It is early in the evening in the backyard of a humble house in a small town in West Texas.

Guapa is the name of a young Latina woman of indigenous descent in her late teens/very early 20s. She has been taken in by a distant family relation of Mexican-Irish background named Roly, after suffering traumatic abuse at the hands of her step-father. Roly is a single mother. She has a daughter and a son—Pepi and Lebon. Both are college-aged and of mixed-race. Guapa lands in this family's lives and serves as a catalyst for all of their aspirations. Guapa's singular dream in life is to become a professional soccer player. She prays to Saint Therese daily to make the dream possible.

In this scene, she shares with Pepi what she imagines her life could be like if her dreams are realized.

GUAPA: Man, I got this whole book-movie in my head 'bout my life that I wanna show the world. In it, I see a huge party, like the *quinceanera* I never had, and I'm wearing a kick-ass poofy dress, that I'd never ever wear, and it's all girly pink and I got roses in my hair, and there are balloons, and cherub boys all naked with silver eye-shadow on.

It's like a pixie dust *quince* and it's also a little Goth, but everybody's into it, you know, everybody's into my party, and there are *futbol* banners everywhere mixed in with the pixie dust and glitter, and all the great players are there from all over—Barcelona and Madrid, Brazil and South

Africa, Mexico and Argentina—and all the saints are there, too. Saint Therese, the Little Flower, is holdin' a soccer ball and smilin' at me, and the land-crossers are dressed up real nice and are askin' the DJ to throw some old songs into the mix—and all the girls are real trad, but in a cool way, and the boys are all angel-like and smooth with no cuts or scars or anything—no suffering on their bodies—on anyone's at this party—and everybody can see us for who we really are—the racist ass-wipes on MLK, the pro scouts, everybody. And we all—all the girls, even the ones who aren't that girly, take the boys out for a spin, while the saints look on and give us a kinda blessin'—Cuz it's like we're under some spell—like outta that movie "Black Swan," but without all the bi-polar freak-out stuff and messed up shit about women havin' to die because they have power—and it's like magic, the real kind, y'know? Cuz everybody can touch us, and no one's scared.

Sometimes when I'm playin', when I'm just kickin' the ball about, I think one day the swan feathers I think I got inside me gonna sparkle so much like crazy Party Town glitter, I'm gonna do a Mardi Gras voodoo incantation, and stir up a party that's gonna take me somewhere else—way the hell outta Texas—and just go.

Half Lives

Peter Tamaribuchi

Act 1. Scene 2. A high school theater in a suburban town. Mid 1980s.

During the height of anti-Japanese sentiment in the 1980s, Justine Fukuyama is a sophomore in high school who just wants to fit in with her almost all white drama department. So she auditions for the role of Ophelia in the school's production of *Hamlet* with a monologue she has written herself.

In this monologue, Justine explores how her obsession with Wonder Woman becomes intertwined with her grief over her mother's death.

JUSTINE: I remember the moment I found out about you, Mom. (*Beat.*) I just got out of sixth grade. I'm in the waiting room, coloring this Super Friends activities book. There wasn't a lot to do those weeks you were in the hospital. Eight long weeks. I remember violently pressing a purple Crayola stub into Wonder Woman's head. (*Beat.*) I look at her eyes: dark and intent as she deflects bullets that are flying towards her. It must be a hell of a job being Wonder Woman. The only female Super Friend. (Except for Zayna, but she's an alien.) Plus, she's also got the skimpiest costume of all the Super Friends. (Well, there's Robin but he doesn't have to wear this thing that makes his breasts look like canons.) She must worry when she's hanging out in the Hall of Justice with all of those guys. (*In Wonder Woman's voice*) "Do they look at me when I'm not paying attention?

Is it hard for them to focus on our mission because I dress like this? Why do I dress like this?

What will happen to me when I get older?
Will it become harder for me to fit into this uniform?
Will I have to retire when that happens?

Will I be all old and wrinkly and sick and…" (*A moment of insecurity and then, a smile.*) "Nah. We, Amazons, live forever." (*Justine goes back to her voice.*)

Dad came in from the waiting room and had this look. Clammy, sunken but no tears. You know he never cries. But he didn't have to say a thing, I just knew. He just put his left hand on my shoulder and squeezed it. Hard. And I started to sob and make a mess of myself so he turned away and… Left. (*She catches herself from crying.*) This is how Men of Steel handle things. (*Beat.*) That night, I had a dream. You're sitting on the edge of my bed, Mom. I can't believe it. You're wearing the complete Wonder costume with red boots and magic lasso. It doesn't look good on you. You're bone thin. The suit hangs on you like wrinkly sheets of flesh. I'm surprised. I figure you at least get a break when you go up there. I was hoping that everyone gets to look wonderful forever and ever. I say, "Mom, what is it really like up there?" You say, "Same as down here. Always trying to save the world and nobody every thanks you." I reach out and I… I want to… (*Beat.*) But then you say, "It's an emergency. There's someone in danger." And before I can touch you, you leap out the window and jump into the invisible jet. Your stick figure rises into the moon's round face, the black edges sinking into the yellow white light, and then it… disappears.

The Happiest Song Plays Last

Quiara Alegría Hudes

Yaz, 30s, Latina, speaks at a community gathering outside City Hall. She delivers a public statement after the unexpected death of Agustín, an elder from the Puerto Rican community in Philadelphia, who was also Yaz's music teacher and closest friend. In addition to a boisterous friendship based in activism, partying, and folkloric music, the two developed a romance in Joaquin's final weeks and attempted to have a child together.

YAZ: Thank you. Miriam Moreno, Agustín's widow, asked me to speak on behalf of the family so they can grieve in privacy. At approximately 4:30 a.m. yesterday Agustín Moreno checked into the Kappa Health Partners emergency room complaining of pain in his left arm. He was told to have a seat and suffered a heart attack within ten minutes of sitting down. For the next hour he sat dead, slumped over in his chair, in full view of the security guard and reception desk. No one lifted a finger. He was finally discovered dead because he was being robbed of his wristwatch and was not resisting. The Mayor's Office and the District Attorney will speak after me and I trust it will not be canned, I trust it will not be, "We take this very seriously etc. and so on." It is time to acknowledge, in detail, the understaffed hospitals, the occupational callousness, the decisions based on ethnic and economic bias, and how no one should ever die like this in the United States of America. Agustín Moreno was a high school guidance counselor, six months short of retiring with pension, and he had health insurance. Kappa Health Partners has no statement at this time? I have prepared a statement for them. This is their <u>second</u> preventable emergency room death this year they took more than half an hour to notice. They have three inpatient deaths currently under investigation including a grandmother who drowned because her tracheotomy had not been cleaned in days.

I can only pray, dear God, that maybe one person is watching, maybe two people are seeing this today, who will continue Agustín's work in the community. Here is what you have to do:

Take your music to people who don't know anything about Puerto Rico or North Philadelphia, and teach.

Take it to 5th and Lehigh and create a festival of Bomba Y Plena.
Take your music to City Hall and take it to Doña Rita's sick bed.

Then grab a hold of a guiro player and go out to the maximum-security prison at Graterford and bring tears of memory and joy to men who made a mistake or are paying for someone else's mistake.

And next time some brass hats decide to play war games on the land of your patria, grab your guitar and jump on the next bus to Lafayette Park by the White House.

And since you will almost always be performing for free, get a job where you can help the young people of our community grow in strength and wisdom.

Then, as a new week starts, stand over by a piano and sing life into your congregation.

And don't forget, after all that, to let us know that you <u>enjoy</u> what you're doing.

My Philadelphia neighbors, we are calling for an immediate boycott of every Kappa Health Partners clinic in the city. Saturday morning outside the Kappa Health emergency room on Olney: it's protest time. Rain or shine, bring your signs. Bring your guitars. Bring your lozenges because we will be heard. What will we have? <u>Survival</u>. When will we demand it? Saturday. See you there.

HappyFlowerNail

Radha Blank

Bed-Stuy, Brooklyn. HappyFlowerNail, a modest nail salon owned by Mrs. Sung.

HappyFlowerNail tells the stories of five women who confront loss, survival, gentrification and the American Dream during one day in a Korean owned nail salon. Mercy, 20s, is a brash, strong-willed young black mother from Bed-Stuy. She is a regular at HappyFlowerNail.

In this monologue, Mercy is flustered as she talks to her favorite aesthetician, Rosa, about her appointment at the Housing Department.

MERCY: Them housing people is full of shit. See, I'm down there, waiting for forever when the lady finally call my number. So I grab TJ and we follow behind her to her desk. I give her my vitals: Mercy Givens, 24, Social Security #, blahblahblah, 2-5-8 Schenectedy Ave #3D. I start to tell her 'bout my trifling landlord when she go on her computer. And she smiling at TJ, "what a beautiful son you got", and I'm like thank you and he flirting with her and they all happy and leprechauns and rainbows and shit, right? Well. She looking at the screen and her face, it turn mad sour, yo. So I'm like "what?!" And she like "Mercy Givens?" And I'm like "Yeah, I just told you!" And she like "Mercy Givens. 258 Schenectedy Ave #3D?" And I'm like "Yeah?!?" And she like "hmmm." And I'm like "hmm what, lady?!" She say "well…this apartment was under lease with Gloria Stubbs." And I'm like "was?" And she like "Gloria Stubbs?" And I'm like "That's my grandmother." And she like "Where your grandmother?" And I'm like "she dead." Lady make that face again… "Well Miss Givens," she say, "looks like your landlord served an eviction notice?" "Eviction notice" she say goin' up on the end with a question mark on it like I know suh-in 'bout that shit! And I'm like "NO." And she like "well—according to this…" but I aint even about to let that bitch finish. "BULLSHIT," I said. And poor TJ start crying cause he see his mommy face and now people crowding around and then TJ—he start wailing and shit. And it hurt to see that shit but I gotta ignore that shit cuz I gotta take care of this shit, you know? I say to the lady "My bad, lady, aight, but that's a damn mistake. I'm Mercy Givens. 258 Schenectedy #3D. I know it ain't my name on that lease…but it's my apartment. My grangran raise me up there from ye high. I aint got no fucking eviction notice…no it ain't possible that it fell off the door…no it ain't possible that that slimy devilspawn landlord slid that shit under my door and I ain't notice it!" Im like "Miss. I'm a upstanding citizen. I got a job. I pay my rent! True! I been late a few times…but…he been tryna get me out on some sneaky shit since my grangran died! You know?!" But she just got her mouth open, looking all scared, prolly cuz I aint never sit back down. And she say all calm…that there ain't nothing she can do. And I'm like "Is you serious!?! You can't help me!? Do you know how long I had to fucking wait for a fucking appointment just to hear you say you can't fucking help me?!!? What I'm 'posed to do?! Where I'm 'posed to go?!?! Huh?!? Lady!?" "Well don't you have anybody?" she say. And I say "Oh, I had somebody…but he died in Afghanistan for your ass and NO we wasn't married…So I can't claim SHIT!" And…all I remember is these big ass security guards come outta nowhere to cart me and my baby out, like I threatened to blow shit up. No. I said I would blow up her desk, that's different. (*beat*) (*Mercy finally breaks down. She holds out her hand to show a broken nail.*) So you could fix this for me?

HappyFlowerNail

Radha Blank

Bed-Stuy, Brooklyn. HappyFlowerNail, a modest nail salon owned by Mrs. Sung.

HappyFlowerNail tells the stories of five women who confront loss, survival, gentrification and the American Dream during one day in a Korean owned nail salon. Mrs. Sung, Korean, 50s, owner and operator of HappyFlowerNail has just been accused of having favoritism for her immigrant workers and not renting one of her upstairs apartments to long time customer, Mercy, because of race.

In this monologue, Mrs. Sung eviscerates Mercy's accusation and reminds her that life has not been easy for any of the women in the shop.

MRS SUNG: Mercy! You don't know the meaning of you name! Cause you Brack!? Cause you BRACK?! That's BULLSHIT Mercy! Mercy! I no gib apartment cause you Brack! I no gib apartment cause you hab no money. Want me to charge what I charge hipster? Look, Lucy, Evelyn, Rosa, Marisol. These girls no free ride. They work for stay upstairs in one apartment! Nonono. Let me talk, KAY?! Cause you Brack! Mrs. Sung need money. You see shop. You see new customer in shop?! NO! They all up block at SUPER POWER NAIL. They heb money. You should ask them for apartment! Why everyone think Mrs. Sung heb money!? Like guy who try to rob 3 time last month! I say, boy, you stupih! Go up block! THEY new shop. They heb money! Cause you Brack! Mercy, I come to dis country with NOTHING. Scrape little money from sell old house in Korea and when I come tru immigration, you know what immigration lady say to me? "Mrs. Sung, you want to lib where? You want to start business WHERE?! Ah! Mrs. Sung, you want to stay safe, you stay out of Brooklyn!" That's what she say to me! I listen Mercy?!?! NO!! Why Because I not scared brack people! Even after guy rob me 3 time! I know dats one brack person not ALL! Cause you brack! How I heb HappyFlowerNail without brack people? Cause you brack! Mercy, I not racist and long time you come here and you say dat bout Mrs. Sung!? (*she's hurt*) Heb same probrem, you know! When I first come dis country, some people no even look me in face when talk-uh to me. So don't you call me hatred brack people, 'kay?! If I hatred brack people, I not let Big Mike sell DbeeD in shop. If I hatred brack people, I not let you yell loud mouth like you do in shop all time! I kick you out. But I no do that. WHY?! I know you looong time, Mercy Gibens. I know you not angry at Mrs. Sung. You just angry at world, at not heb family, angry at lose son father in stupid war. But Mercy, Mrs. Sung get angry too. I tired of lose money. I tired of Super Power Nail. I tired of Rosa leave. I tired of get rob. I tired lose respect. I tired be called racist Mercy! (*She pulls the paper out of her pocket.*) Well. Maybe I not be tired no more. Maybe you no have to call immigration on shop because…maybe…just maybe I let shop go. Okay?!

In the Continuum

Nikkole Salter

Scene 9. A popular restaurant in Los Angeles, CA, 2004.

In the Continuum is a play of parallel stories that follows two women—Nia in Los Angeles, CA, USA, and Abigail in Harare, Zimbabwe—over the course of one weekend from the moment they receive news of their pregnancy and HIV+ status, to their first moment of attempted disclosure.

In this monologue Miss Keysha (aka Keyshawn)—a transgender African American male in his early twenties—responds to his younger cousin Nia's request for advice with respect to her new pregnancy.

MISS KEYSHA: (*to the waiter*) No, the water is fine. But could you bring some lemon. And sugar. No, I don't want lemonade. Did I ask for lemonade? If I wanted lemonade I would order lemonade. Thank you.

(*to Nia*) Okay. So, should you have his baby? Should you have his baby? Should a dope fiend in a crack house run from the police? Hell yeah, you should have his baby.

(*to himself*) What's takin' him so long. (*to the waiter*) Waiter!

(*to Nia*) No, I don't, Nia. I really don't see what the dilemma is. It's not like you got pregnant by some ole, dirty, jerry curl juicy, gold-tooth pimp. It ain't like you don't know who the daddy is. We talkin' Darnell Smith. Dar-nell Smith. The crem de la crem. Do you know how many girls pokin' needles in condoms tryin'ta have his baby. And here you sit, on the come-up like Mary pregnant with Jesus, talkin' 'bout should you have his baby. Have

Miss Keysha taught you nothin'? What else you gonna do? That's Darnell Smith's baby and everybody know Darnell Smith. And these recruiters is lickin' his anus tryin' to get him to go to they school. I'm talking UCLA, Notre Damé. Indian-I-A, all of 'em. And you know what's gonna happen when he get outta school. He goin' straight to the NBA. Do you know what that mean? Do you know what that mean? That mean you…we about to be set for life. For LIFE. I'm talkin' Malibu mansion. Mercedes Benz. SL class on Sprewells! I'm talkin' Louis Vetton luggage…no, no, no. Real Louis Vetton luggage. VIP parties, backstage passes…hold on. (*he has an orgasm*) Ooooo! I can't believe I gave him to you. He was right on the line, he coulda went either way, either way. I was the one introduced ya'll when you was eight cuz I was tired of you followin' me around. Uhh huh. Those were my dark days of darkness—before I became the fine specimen you see before you. We was all staying' wit Auntie Gina—all of us up in that one room; and her makin' me take you with me when I went out, knowin' you would tell if I did somethin' wrong. Why you think I'd have you to go play with Darnell? To get yo' nosey ass out my business. Who knew Darnell would end up a damn star? He about to be so rich. I shoulda went ahead and did him then, with his little eight year old pee pee. (*acting out what that might look and sound like*) Speakin' of pee-pee. I gotta go tinkle.

(*to himself*) Where is my water and lemons. Where is the damn complimentary bread? I tell you, that waiter got three mo' minutes—

(*to Nia*) Stop lookin' so sad. You not dyin', the world ain't over. You ain't the first one to end up pregnant. You should be happy! 'Cuz, you rollin' in the game with the big dogs now WOOF, WOOF! But let me warn you: this is not high school—these girls will be after Darnell and these bitches is ruthless. Don't trust none of 'em. They would fuck yo' man and yo' daddy in the same day. I've seen it happen: sports will turn these men into fools, but it'll turn women into…—Halle Berry in 'Jungle Fever': (*mocking*) "Can I suck yo' dick? No? Uh, can I suck yo' dick? Anybody dick? Everybody dick?" Just wait 'til he get a little money, a little more fame—I already see that nigga every weekend with his hand indiscriminately placed between somebody's legs. And them girls! Please! They love it. Well, they may cum, but they will go cuz they ain't shit to him. You got his baby. You stayin'. But it won't be easy. 'Cuz he'll be out with two, three of 'em at the same time every night and won't think nothin'of it. Then he'll bring you back some nastiness, his PR person will get involved and the next thing you know, you readin' about how you tried to give it to him to bribe him outta some money or somethin'. Hell yeah, we want to be paid and pampered, but not enough to be catchin' no STD. You remember my roommate Monica?

Monica. You know, (*imitates Monica sucking her thumb*) Yeah her.

(*with discretion*) She had Chlamydia. Girl, yes! Walkin' around with it, thought it was a damn yeast infection. By the time she asked me to help her to the clinic, she couldn't even walk. And when she got there they said she had waited so long it turned into P-I-D—Pussy in Distress, yes. She got that shit from Jerry—that muthafucka didn't even know he had it. He coulda been walkin' around with herpes, shit, AIDS and not even know it. Of course she was afraid to tell him! I had to confront his punk ass and you know what he said? He said, "I don't know whatchu talkin' 'bout. That's on her," like she gave it to herself. That nigga was on the DL, had Chla-my-di-a and he was still tryin' to make it seem like it was all on her. Like she did it like all by herself. How you even do that? What, you be like (*she imitates what giving herself a sexually transmitted disease would look like*)– Okay, okay, okay. The point is this: These men don't give a fuck about you. All you are to them is a piece of ass. And I'ma be damned if I'ma let my cousin get used up and then end up with nothin'. If you're givin' it up, then you best believe he givin' it up too. And you sho' ain't havin' no babies for free. That is not prostitution, that's called takin' care-a you. I mean, look-atcha mama! She dated some first class Negroes, had they baby, but still couldn't pay her rent. The last thing you wanna be is some hood-rat, baby-mama, walkin' around with cold sores and house shoes; buyin' government cheese with food stamps when yo' baby daddy in the N-B fuckin' A, and playin' husband to some other bitch and her kids. Then who the one lookin' stupid? Now, at least if you his wife, you get half, even if he divorce your ass; even if you do get Chlamydia. Then, whatever way it go, you won't never have to worry about money, and can do whatever the fuck you wanna do. Write your poetry, be Maya Angelou, whatever.

Listen to me: Don't let that boy out your sight. Remind him that you was the one at his games before anybody knew his name. Tell his mama you carrying his baby. Mmm—hum. Naw, go 'head, make it a family affair. Didn't you say you met her at they family picnic?

See! She probably already like you! And once you have her, it don't matter what he say. Don't stop 'til you get keys to the crib and a ring on that finger! Should you have his baby…how else you gon' pay me back for all the shit I did for you? Nia, havin' a baby is a blessing. I mean, think about it. I look better than all ya'll heifers put together, but I cannot have a baby out my ding-a-ling.

Whatever you do, I'ma always be your cousin, but remember, we already live in hell. Don't do nothin' so you have to spend eternity there too. God gave you that baby. That baby is yo' ticket out. (*she exits*)

Last Dance

Brenda Wong Aoki

Act 2. Scene 5. The living room in a small house in a working class neighborhood of San Jose California, 1998.

An elderly Nisei woman and her husband who were both interned in Japanese Prison Camps during WWII. Their home is a maze of newspapers, Costco runs, and gifts from Wal-Mart for grand-children, great grand children and the occasional visitor. They sit in the only two empty chairs in the house offering *arare*, Japanese rice crackers to the audience. The old man, wearing a faded Hawaiian shirt, is silent throughout his wife's monologue but nods his head in agreement with everything she says, smiling like a Buddha. After several hours of pleasantries, the old woman finally feels comfortable enough to tell her story.

In this monologue, the woman reveals a tragedy that happens on the train ride to Poston Prison Camp and how it continues to haunt her to this day.

ANONYMOUS NISEI WOMAN: I am a U.S. citizen. My father fought in World War I. My brothers were *drafted* and fought in World War II. I am a nurse. Still am—This year, we've helped so many friends die... I'm 85, my husband's 87. So we think it's time we tell this story.

It's about the train ride...

We were newly weds, with a week old baby and a house full of brand new furniture. We had one week to sell everything. We got $50 bucks. We went down to the train station with mostly just the baby stuff and the clothes on our backs. When we got there, soldiers were everywhere. They separated the men from the women. The windows of the train were blacked out and nailed shut. I was put in the car with all the mothers and babies and this is what I want to tell you. I see my friend Michi. She and I had just had our babies together over at General only Michi's baby was so sick—the doctors said he would *die* if he left the hospital. So Michi got on that train *without* her baby. *Kowai sou...*

But just as we were about to leave the station, soldiers come and dump a baby on one of the empty seats. All the women wondered, "Whose baby? Whose baby?" Do you know it was Michi's baby?!! The soldiers had taken him out of the hospital *against* doctor's orders and just dumped him on a seat! So Michi sat next to me because like I told you, I am a nurse. I took one look at that baby... Its cry was *so* weak!

Now Dr. Takeshita—the doctor I worked for, was in the next car and he told me if anything should happen to one of the mothers or the babies to go get him. So at the next stop, I got off the train. But a soldier pointed a bayonet at me.

I said "A baby is sick...A baby may be *dying*!"
He just shoved that bayonet toward my belly and yelled,
"The next one goes right through you!"

I got back on the train. It was so hot in there, with all the windows shut. We didn't know where we were going and they only fed us once; spoiled milk and green baloney just left on the platform like we were animals or something.

With nothing to drink, our breast milk was drying up and everybody's babies were crying and crying! Whooooheee! But Michi's baby was so quiet. Then I realized it was dead. But Michi didn't seem to notice. I mean she *knew*, but she just...(*Michi rocks and sings her mama song...*)

When we finally arrived, we were in the middle of nowhere. The desert. We are city people. We never been to a place like that.

In all the commotion, Michi slipped away. They couldn't find her for hours! They had to get a jeep to go get her! There she was—walking through in the desert with her dead baby in her arms. *Looking for a hospital.*

My breast milk never came back and my baby would have died too because all she had those first few weeks in camp was sugar water. But Mac, the *Hakujin* pharmacist back home, heard about my situation and sent me formula the whole time. A white guy! Never charged us nothing. My daughter's had health problems her whole life because of that time, but she survived.

55 years have come and gone...

My husband's cousin married Michi's cousin, so he sees her from time to time at family functions. But me, I can't come. She won't see me.

You see...my face reminds her of that train ride.

Lidless

Frances Ya-Chu Cowhig

Act 1. Scene 1. An interrogation room at the Guantanamo Bay deten-
tion center. Cuba, 2004.

Alice is a 25 year-old woman from Texas. She is also a highly trained U.S.
army interrogator in the last week of her tour of duty at Guantanamo.
She is sleep-deprived, and has been popping beta-blockers like candy.
She has been interrogating Bashir, a Pakistani-Canadian detainee, for
days without progress, and is about to try a new tactic, 'Invasion of
Space by a Female,' that exploits her knowledge of the detainee's religion
to 'break' him.

ALICE: Hey now. For a second there, with the light on you like that, you
looked like my Lucas. Call me overworked and underfucked, but from
where I'm standing, y'all could be cousins. I'm touching myself. My fingers trail up my thigh as I think of all our bodies could do. I could sink onto
your hard, hot cock. I could bury my face in your neck. You could hold me.
You could move me. You could help me find light and redemption and
peace. What's the matter, Mo? Is the great Islamic sword too weary to
rise today? (*Beat.*) Holy mother. Looks like I found your sweet spot. Right
here. An inch beneath your left ear. Jesus. I could hang Old Glory on that
pole. What are we going to do about that boner?

(*Alice flinches. She wipes invisible spit off her face.*)

Now, now. The only spittin' allowed is the kind that comes from down
there. Besides. You like this. Our heads and hearts try to trick us, but

our bodies never lie. Roll with me, baby. Don't fight. Give it up, sweet pea. Stop your prayin'. If Allah was in Gitmo, we'd have him in solitary, so he wouldn't be able to hear you anyway. (*Beat.*) I forgot to tell you, I'm bleeding, and there's nothing shielding you from my twenty-five-year-old cunt, just red, red, red, stainin' skin already caked pus white and blue with bruises, making you the color of the flag I've sworn to protect. I've read about your hell. Your silence condemns you to that furnace fueled by the flesh of men, where walls are fire, smoke's the only shade, and the only beverage is the blood bubbling through your burning skin. Stay silent and my blood will damn your veins, so you better hope to Allah there's no such thing as eternity.

(*Alice takes off her shirt, revealing a lacy red push-up bra.*)
Last chance.

A Life in Knots

L'xeis' Diane E. Benson

Scene 2. A Congressman's office in December, the last day before holiday break. It is war time.

Jessie is a Native American mother of one child; a son serving in the Army who was severely wounded in a war prompted by the United States. Western and tribally educated, she appreciates her culture and thus values the role of the warrior. Incensed by the irony that Native Americans serve in higher numbers per capita in the Armed Forces than most yet are sent into combat by representatives whose children don't serve, Jessie and her accomplice seek to confront their state's Congressman. The souvenir photo the Congressman takes with her, as he does with every visitor, sets her off. Feigning a happy visit, she lingers as the Congressman excuses his staff for the holidays. Alone with the aging Congressman, Jessie and Benjamin capture and tie him to a chair. Feeling control after feeling so powerless for so long, she stuffs a sock in the Congressman's mouth and proceeds to "educate" him on his responsibility to warriors, while finally unleashing her rage.

JESSIE: I am not prepared today to debate the philosophical and ideological possibilities of a world without wars, but that is not to say we shouldn't… (*squeezes his cheeks*).

Imagine there's no heaven, it's easy if you try, no hell below us, above us, only sky. Imagine all the people, living life in peace…

Noooo. No speaking. (*duct-taping his mouth*).

My son's been fighting in a war I find wrong and immoral. The next logical conclusion does not require me to hate my son. He is just one of the foot soldiers. Do we say to the soldier, you are wrong and immoral? Would that be right? No. The century's old military system molds them through discipline and rigorous training to act on behalf of a nation or grouping of people. Am I right Congressman? Shake your head yes, or no. Come on now. Yes or no? Good boy.

By training a warrior, we ask them to act through some aggressive means on our behalf. A warrior is not someone who acts on his own accord, or his own ideas. He is trusting that he acts for the good of his group, his nation. It is the nation's responsibility to make sure that the WHY of a warrior's actions is just. This way, the warrior need only busy himself with the task requested of him. My son got busy, doing what you voted for. But what if you are wrong and immoral? Huh? Your kids aren't busy are they? Are you proud of those precious kids going to Ivy League this year? Just like nothing was going on? No war. Nobody getting killed. No getting their fucking legs blown off. (*she smashes his family picture*).

Now Congressman. Eddie. Can I call you Eddie? Our Troops trust that we will only send them in harm's way for thought-out and necessary causes. We Hold That Trust. You. You and me. It is important that we clearly understand that. It lies on these American shoulders. But somebody didn't do their job. We have to Vote with them in mind, to Advocate with them in mind, to Convene with them in mind, to choose to fight for what's right, with them in mind, to be truly just, with them in mind. These are our sons, our daughters. These are OUR Warriors. But how many of you 500 members of Congress has a child at war huh?

You talk about making sacrifices, but what are YOUR sacrifices? (*writing on his face "son"*). It is my son, my neighbor's daughter, the waiter's kids; these are the people who serve our society as warriors. When we do not Vote we break that sacred trust. When we play politics with their lives, their family's lives, their neighbor's lives, we break that trust. When we vote in imbeciles who LIE to them, we break that trust! (*stabs his leg with the pen*)

Thousands of soldiers have been wounded. Thousands without legs or arms. Soldiers are coming home with diseases, including a parasitic sand fly that quite literally eats humans alive. Even the treatment is deadly. It's true. There was an article in the Ft. Campbell Courier about it. You never heard of the Ft. Campbell Courier? Why would you? That's for Army guys and their families. You did what? Served two years back in the 50s? No war for you.

And your TV ad says how you support the military families. I'm a family of a soldier. How do like me now? Do you support me now? It's amazing isn't it? How mothers and fathers of soldiers receive no assistance to get through all this shit. Their kid gets blown up, and see what happens? Just look at what happens! (*hits his bleeding leg*)

(*She ties a yellow ribbon in his hair*). We are waaaay too quiet and polite. What is that kind of silence? I can't hear you. Is it fear? Is fear a part? You tell me. Is it fear?

A Local Perspective

Tammy Haili'ōpua Baker

Kahalu'u, on this island of O'ahu, Hawai'i. A typical *'ohana* (family) style party is underway in Local Aunty's backyard.

Through a series of linked monologues, this play shares the opinions and life experiences of individuals born and raised in Hawai'i, commonly referred to as locals. Local Sista is a 30-something woman who begins to analyze different phenomena and codes of conduct in her community.

In this monologue Local Sista reflects on the female anatomy. She makes light of local terminology used to reference the vagina and grounds her beliefs in Hawaiian cultural practice.

LOCAL SISTA: You know, growing up here in Hawai'i, we no really refer to our dakine as our vagina. That's one foreign word for most local households. We probably only hear that word in sixth grade sex-ed, when our teacher was trying to educate us about the penis and vagina relationship and function.

I can remember all us girls looking at each other, surprised at the topic of discussion, we leaned in for more information while the boys just made boto jokes in the back. (*Imitating Natural Vibes song.*) Boto boto suksuk, boto boto suuuk. All 'ono for themselves talking about oofing.

Anyway, depending on what kind of household you grew up in, you learned different terminology for your dakine. Wait, let's clarify dakine... dakine is a common reference word for something that me as the speaker assumes that you as the listener knows what I'm referring to, so I no just have to say 'um. Previously established content.

Where I was, oh yeah different cultural names for your dakine. There's ching-ching. Ching-ching, like when you play store, $3.99, $4.99, ching-ching.

So…your choney, choch, the chocho, your bean, the funas, the beegee, your bilat, your nani, the pua. People say punani. Punani Patrol, what you think Del Beazley was thinking about when he wrote that song. My mom would say, "Go wash your guavas." After going beach my aunty used to tell us girls, "When you 'au'au wash good down there now, you no like the sand in your dakine make pearls."

All this obsession with cleanliness. Wash your nani. Clean that ching-ching. Wash your dakine.

Ever notice how quickly we make references to bad smells down there in order to make derogatory comments about women we no like or just to tease one another. Smelly bean, that was a popular one in high school. "You did your homework or what, smelly bean?" What about stink ho… "She's a stink ho, I don't know why you friends with her!" "Stink bilat!" Or when that girl who was flirting with your cousin came into the class-room… "Rotten tuna, she better stay away from my cousin." "Eh, no open your legs, what's that smell, nato?"

When it comes to smell, how can we forget our ma'i. Girl, where does that stuff come from??? And she flow! Getting your ma'i every month may be a part of womanhood that I can appreciate today but, BRAH it was a bitch in high school. Especially when you on your rags and you leak through your clothes and what not. And then you gotta figure out how you going hide 'um. With your jacket maybe, or ask your friend if she get extra shorts. Everybody could tell you was on your rags.

Getting back to the term ma'i. Ma'i in Hawaiian is one way of saying you're ill or sick like a dog. Make sense? Ma'i is also the term for genitals, your dakine. Male and female same term. Traditionally Hawaiians cele-brated and honored the ma'i with song compositions. Every event was closed with a mele ma'i, this continues today. Anyway we have more spe-cific terminology for the various parts of the male and female ma'i. For instance, the kohe. The kohe is not usually seen unless your pants give you camel toe. Revealing the lips, ninja boot action. Eh, some wahine like that. If you never figure 'um out yet, kohe is the vagina.

Ladies, the power of the kohe is undeniable. The ma'i is something to be celebrated. So tonight and always treat your nani right, tend to her, listen to her, celebrate her, love her, honor her. Love your dakine! Mahalo!

Mariela in the Desert

Karen Zacarias

When is Art a Lie? Mariela and José were once the golden couple of the Mexican artists' inner circle. Together they built a family and an artist colony to host friends Diego Rivera, Frida Kahlo, and Rufino Tamayo. But now their daughter has grown up and run away, their friends are too famous to call, and artistic inspiration has been strangled by isolation and lies. Set in the northern Mexican desert in 1950, *Mariela in the Desert* is a deadly mystery—a layered yet profoundly honest story of what happens to a family when creativity is forced to dry and wither away.

In this monologue, Mariela (aged 38–45), a mother and former painter, living in a failed art colony in the desert, tells her talented artistic 12-year-old daughter Blanca, a lie that is a truth.

MARIELA: When I was twelve years old, my parents owned a large factory outside Monterrey. We lived in a grand house; my father bred fine horses while my fancy mother tried to breed me into a fine lady. But one day…I took my mother's favorite brooch. It had a red ruby in the middle and twelve Colombian emeralds all around. It was very expensive but I thought the red and green looked quite awful together…so I spent the entire afternoon prying the emeralds out.

That night, my mother discovered the brooch was missing and she and my father threatened horrible things to whoever was the thief. So I hid her broken brooch and said nothing. Two days later, my sweet nanny suddenly stopped coming. My parents had turned her into the police for stealing the brooch. After that, things happened. My nanny's family plotted revenge and the factory had a terrible fire. Unable to pay his debts, my father grew ill as the bank came and claimed the horses, the house, the furniture, the jewels, my toys…everything! People said we were cursed.

(*Beat*)

But not me. The ruby paid for my art school. And I sold the emeralds to buy my wedding dress. And I never had to be a fine lady again. (*Beat*) Choose what you inherit very carefully.

Marisol

José Rivera

New York City. The Present. Winter.

Marisol is an apocalyptic play in which apples are extinct, God is aging, men are having babies and the Bronx is a war zone. Marisol Perez, a 26-year-old Puerto Rican woman, is a copy editor for a Manhattan publisher. Although she has elevated herself into a white-collar existence, she continues to live alone in her dangerous childhood neighborhood of the Bronx. At the top of the play, Marisol barely flees an attack by a crazed man with a golf club while commuting on the subway. Later that evening Marisol is visited by the Angel of the Lord.

In this monologue, Marisol speaks to the Angel of the Lord and is afforded the opportunity to ask her most burning questions.

MARISOL: Are you real? Are you true? Are you gonna make the Bronx safe for me? Are you gonna make miracles and reduce my rent? Is it true angels' favorite food is Thousand Island dressing? Is it true your shit smells like mangoes and when you're drunk you speak Portuguese?!...

Wait a minute—am I dead? Did I die tonight? How did I miss that? Was it the man with the golf club? Did he beat me to death? Oh my God. I've been dead all night. And when I look around I see that Death is my ugly apartment in the Bronx. No this can't be Death! Death can't have this kind of furniture!...

Am I pregnant with the Lord's baby?! Is the new Messiah swimming in my electrified womb? Is the supersperm of God growing a mythic flower deep in the secret greenhouse inside me? Will my morning sickness taste like communion wine? This is amazing—*billions* of women on earth, and I get knocked up by God!…

No. Then what is it? Are you real or not? 'Cause if you're real and God is real and the Gospels are real, this would be the perfect time to tell me. 'Cause I once looked for angels, I did, in every shadow of my childhood— but I never found any. I thought I'd find you hiding inside the notes I sang to myself as a kid. The songs that put me to sleep and kept me from killing myself with fear. But I didn't see you then. C'mon! Somebody up there has to tell me why I live the way I do! What's going *on* here, anyway? Why is there a war on children in this city? Why are apples extinct? Why are they planning to drop human insecticide on overpopulated areas of the Bronx? Why has the color blue disappeared from the sky? Why does common rainwater turn your skin bright red? Why do cows give salty milk? Why did the Plague kill half my friends? AND WHAT HAPPENED TO THE MOON? Where did the moon go? How come nobody's seen it in nearly *nine months…?*

Miss Lead

Mary Kathryn Nagle

Act 2. Scene 1. Joplin, Missouri, early 1990s.

Rebecca, citizen of the Quapaw Tribe of Oklahoma, is around 50 years old. Katie McCartney is 18 and sick. After just one semester away at college, she is forced to return to the family home in the Tri-State Mining District to grapple with a debilitating illness. Rebecca is a nurse in the town hospital, and a member of the Quapaw Tribe in Oklahoma. During World War II, Katie's grandfather (who owned the Tri-State Mining District) obtained authorization from the Bureau of Indian Affairs to—without the consent of the Tribe—mine lead for bullets on the Quapaw reservation. As a result, Rebecca's community and tribe have been wracked with illness and loss.

While in the hospital, Katie meets Rebecca, who encourages her to reclaim her own Native American roots. In this scene, Rebecca helps Katie learn that her illness and her identity are inextricably woven into the soil of the land and history of this country.

REBECCA: To say you're Native means that you acknowledge you shouldn't be here today. To be Native means that at some point along the way, this Government tried to kill your mother, your father, or your grandma or your grandpa, and although the United States was successful in killing 99% of us, somehow your grandma was a part of the 1 percent that survived. My grandma talked about the Miami. You know the Quapaw, we were here first. Got moved over to Indian territory earlier than the rest, except the Cherokee. And so a lot of tribes that were moved here after the Civil War were placed first on our reservation, until the Government figured out what it wanted to do with them. My great-grandma was alive when the Miami arrived. She told my grandma that when the army marched them over the Kansas state line and onto our reservation, they numbered less than a hundred. Just a century ago they were a nation of more than ten thousand, but by the time they made it down here on their final Trail of Tears, only 100 survived. Your great-grandma was one of those 100. So you don't have to be Native. You can forget where your great-grandma came from, you can abandon her culture, her customs, her prayers, her ceremony, your heritage. And you can certainly pass for white. If that's what you want to do. But when you do, just know that you're only helping the United States accomplish what it couldn't quite finish one hundred years ago.

The Mountaintop

Katori Hall

Room 306 at The Lorraine Motel in Memphis, TN. April 3, 1968.

The Mountaintop explores a fictitious encounter between Dr. Martin Luther King, Jr. and a beautiful young hotel maid, Camae, the day before the Civil Rights Movement leader's assassination. As the play progresses, it is revealed that Camae is not actually a hotel maid, but an angel sent by God to prepare Dr. King for his impending death.

In this scene, and in attempts to help Dr. King embrace his martyrdom, Camae opens up about her former life, proving that although she is a messenger from God, even angels are not perfect.

CAMAE: You perfect?...Then why should I be? Honey, I've robbed. I've lied. I've cheated. I've failed. I've cursed. But what I'm ashamed of most is I've hated. Hated myself. Sacrificed my flesh so that others might feel whole again. I thought it was my duty. All that I had to offer this world.

What else was a poor black woman, the mule of the world, here for? Last night, in the back of a alley I breathed my last breath. A man clasped his hands like a necklace 'round my throat. I stared into his big blue eyes, as my breath got ragged and raw, and I saw the Hell this old world had put him through. The time he saw his father hang a man. The time he saw his mother raped. I felt so sorry for him. I saw what the world had done to him, and I still couldn't forgive. I hated him for stealing my breath. When I passed on to the other side, God—ooooo, she is more gorgeous than me. She the color of midnight and her eyes are brighter than the stars.

Her hair...well...just you wait til you see her hair—God stood there before me. With this look on her face. I just knowed she was just soooo disappointed in me. I was just a' cryin' weepin' at her feet. Beggin' her not to throw me down. All that sinnin'. All that grime on my soul. All that hatred in my heart. But then I looked up and saw that She was smilin' down at me. She opened her mouth, and silence came out. But I heard her loud and clear. "I got a special task for you and if you complete it, all your sins will be washed away."

I opened my file. And I saw my task was you. What could little old me, give to big old you? I thought you was gone be perfect. Well, you ain't, but then you are. You have the biggest heart I done ever knownt. You have the strength to love those who could never love you back. If I had just a small fraction of the love you have for this world, then maybe, just maybe I could become half the angel you are.

N(E)IG(H)G(BO)ERS

Branden Jacobs-Jenkins

Scene 6. An upper middle class neighborhood in suburban America. The present.

N(e)ig(h)g(bo)ers is a wildly theatrical, explosive play on race. The unconventional comedy uses minstrelsy to explore the history of black theatre, and to confront tensions in 'post-racial' America. When the minstrel Crow family moves into the neighborhood, interracial couple Richard and Jean Patterson, are forced to deal with the implications of their changing neighborhood.

In this monologue, Melody Patterson, a bi-racial teen, berates her parents after her father humiliated her in school. She channels Ms. Fun during quotations, who is shrewd, Asian-accented.

MELODY: Yes! And she's a bitch and she hates me and has me sit in the front of the class, so she always knows when I'm late, like today, because I walked to school and I'm such a fat cow, so I'm a slow walker, and I'm not even in my chair good when I can see Ms. Fun like reaching for her tardy slips when Dad stalks in, doesn't even say anything, and just marches right up to my seat, grabs me by arm like some sort prostitute, and yanks me out of the classroom, and starts yelling at me, yelling at me in the hall with this terrible echo so the whole school can just like hear him shouting Rape and Countryfolk and Self-Respect and Socioeconomics and Class Difference and Barack Obama and Crack and Teen Pregnancy and People Trying to Pull You Down and all these heads start poking out of doorways, and I just wanted to die, Mom. I wanted to die!

…Oh my god! She couldn't even look at me once the entire rest class. She just stood there with this look on her face like "Oh my god. Oh my god. I am terrified. Some Negro man just come in to my classroom and snatch away one of my student. But wait! Wait! Crazy Negro man appear to be her father!" No one could look at me. Because all these white girls are like flipping their hair and whispering about the girl with the psycho crazy freak of father and tomorrow—oh my god, I can't go to school tomorrow! And do you know why? Because you are a monster and I hate you and if I could I would kill you for doing this! I would kill you and then I would kill myself!

A Nice Indian Boy

Madhuri Shekar

Scene 10: Evocation. The final scene of the play. The dressing room of an Indian marriage hall in San Jose, CA. Present day.

A Nice Indian Boy is a dramedy about an Indian-American family grappling with questions of marriage, love and commitment across generations and cultures. The story begins with Naveen, 31, bringing home his fiancé Keshav to meet his parents. Although Naveen's parents, Archit and Megha, have just about made peace with the fact that their son is gay, the fact that he now wants to get married is an entirely different matter altogether. To make this more complicated, their older daughter Arundhathi, 33, suddenly arrives back home to announce that she's getting divorced.

In the final scene, Megha (late 50s), Naveen and Arundhathi are getting ready for Naveen and Keshav's wedding. Naveen is feeling last-minute wedding jitters, and Arundhathi is still hurting over her failing marriage. When Megha's kids ask her how *her* marriage—an arranged marriage—has survived all these years, she comes up with a surprising story.

MEGHA: It was difficult in the beginning. All marriages are. You're trying to feel each other out, figure out what the other person likes, doesn't like, prefers, doesn't prefer, REALLY likes, REALLY doesn't like, how much, how many times...

It was embarrassing. I was so nervous. Do you know I'd never done it before marriage?

Yes, yes, I'm talking about cooking! So. I tried making him idlis for our first breakfast. I thought it would be nice, because he grew up in the South. It came out like...idli pudding. He had to eat it with a spoon.

(*getting emotional*) The memories are still so fresh.

(*collecting herself*) Anyway. It went on like this for a week. Dosas falling apart into pieces. Daal like water. Potatoes so tough, they could chip your teeth. Then finally one night—I woke up in the middle of the night and the whole house smelled of this incredible aroma! I went into the kitchen, and your father was making—so much food! Aloo paratha, daal makhani, navratan kurma, bhindi curry—RamaKrishnaHari—he was even making gulab jamun. The poor man just couldn't take it anymore! He was starving—he needed to eat! He was so apologetic, but I was thrilled. I sat down, and he served me, and we ate and we ate and we ate until the sun came up! And then we did it.

Yes, yes, more cooking.
I never had to cook again in my life!

Night over Erzinga

Adriana Sevahn Nichols

Act 2. Scene 8.

Alice Oghidanian is found wandering on Elm Street, barefoot, in her nightgown, carrying an empty suitcase. Thus begins this ancestor play where, a granddaughter's need to know the story of her family, unearths the truth. Alice and Ardavazt, both the sole survivors of their families, murdered during the Armenian Genocide of 1915, meet, and marry in Worcester, Massachusetts. Ardavazt works hard to build them a future while Alice is haunted by the past. Alice begins to unravel emotionally as their daughter turns eight, the age Alice's sister was when she was killed. On this night, in 1938, Alice will not be silenced. Ardavazt tries to stop her, "I will not let you bring that river of blood into my house! If you can't let the past die then what good was it to have survived?"

In this monologue, Alice reveals the horror of what happened to her family in front of her eyes. She is unable to carry the guilt of not being able to save her sister any longer.

ALICE: What do you know of survival?? You witnessed none of it. You got on a boat, came here with money in your pockets, and one day the letters stopped coming from home. THAT IS NOT SURVIVAL. I was fourteen when the soldiers came to my village. We left the bread still baking in the toneer. The clothes drying on the line. We thought we were coming back. My mother smeared my face and dress with dirt and commanded me to keep my eyes down as we were marched into the desert. My parents were so terrified of me being taken, at night, like the other girls, they would bury me, up to my neck, in the cold night sand. One night, I heard my father yelling with the soldiers. My mother took off her scarf and covered my face. The ground shook as the black boots came towards my body. My father pleaded with the soldiers—"No—she's just a child—please-no-my God-please," but it wasn't me they were coming for. They hadn't buried my sister, Anoush, because at eight, they thought she was too young to be of any interest to the soldiers. Anoush screamed as they pulled her away from my father. My mother ripped open her own dress—begging them to take her instead. The soldiers held onto my father as they cut off my mother's head. My father vomited and they kicked him. He was shaking and crying and praying. They held him down while three soldiers surrounded Anoush and spread her legs open with their bayonets. My father screamed a sound I had never heard him make before. I held my breath—too afraid to make the fabric of my mother's scarf move—I held my breath—like when we would go to the Black Sea, every summer, and I would scare mother by how long I could stay under water. "Alice, Alice," she'd say, "Enough, your mother's heart!" "Dikran," she'd yell, "Your daughter is drowning," and Papa would jump into the water and come find me. I wanted to shout "Anoush, kick them, bite them, you must fight!" But I just held my breath—I watched Anoush's legs tremble as each one took their turn on her, and then after a while...her legs just stopped moving. I lay there in the sandy grave, my family's blood all around me for hours...days...willing God to drown me in that river.

Ruined

Lynn Nottage

Early 2000s. A mining town in the Democratic Republic of Congo. Mama Nadi's bar and brothel.

"In the Congo" where "things slip from our fingers like butter", Salima, a pregnant Hema girl in her late teens/early twenties, struggles to maintain hope for a brighter future. Having been shunned by her husband and village due to her abduction and rape by multiple soldiers, she finds herself employed in one of the last vestiges of safety in the war torn land—Mama Nadi's bar and brothel. Despite the atrocities committed against Salima, she still hopes for reconciliation with her husband.

In this monologue, Salima reveals how she was captured and what she endured at the hands of the rebel soldiers.

SALIMA: Do you know what I was doing on that morning? (*A calm washes over Salima*).

I was working in our garden picking the last of the sweet tomatoes. I put Beatrice down in the shade of a Frangipani tree, because my back was giving me some trouble. Forgiven? Where was Fortune? He was in town fetching a new iron pot. "Go," I said "Go, today man or you won't have dinner tonight!" I had been after him for a new pot for a month. And finally on that day the damn man had to go and get it. A new pot. The sun was about to crest, but I had to put in another hour before it got too hot. It was such a clear and open sky. This splendid bird, a peacock had come into the garden to taunt me, and was showing off its feathers. I stooped down and called to the bird. "Wssht, Wssht." And I felt a shadow cut across my back, and when I stood four men were there over me, smiling, wicked school boy smiles. "Yes?" I said. And the tall soldier slammed the butt of his gun into my cheek. Just like that. It was so quick, I didn't even know I'd fallen to the ground. Where did they come from? How could I not have heard them?... One of the soldiers held me down with his foot. He was so heavy, thick like an ox and his boot was cracked and weathered like it had been left out in the rain for weeks. His boot was pressing my chest and the cracks in the leather had the look of drying sorghum. His foot was so heavy and it was all I could see, as the others... "took" me. My baby was crying. She was a good baby. Beatrice never cried, but she was crying, screaming. "Shhh" I said. "Shhh." And right then... (*Salima closes her eyes.*)

A soldier stomped on her head with his boot. And she was quiet. (*A moment. Salima releases*)

Where was everybody? WHERE WAS EVERYBODY?!... I fought them!... I did!... But they still took me from my home. They took me through the bush, raiding thieves. Fucking demons! "She is for everyone, soup to be had before dinner," that is what someone said. They tied me to a tree by my foot, and the men came whenever they wanted soup. I make fires, I cook food, I listen to their stupid songs, I carry bullets, I clean wounds, I wash blood from their clothing, and, and, and... I lay there as they tore me to pieces, until I was raw...five months. Five months. Chained like a goat. These men fighting... fighting for our liberation. Still I close my eyes and I see such terrible things. Things, I cannot stand to have in my head. How can men be this way?

(*A moment*)

It was such a clear and open sky. So, so beautiful. How could I not hear them coming?

A peacock wandered into my garden, and the tomatoes were ripe beyond belief.

Our fields of red sorghum were so perfect, it was going to be a fine season.

Fortune thought so too, and we could finally think about planning a trip on the ferry to visit his brother. Oh God please give me back that morning. "Forget the pot, Fortune. Stay,"... "Stay," that's what I would tell him. What did I do, Sophie? I must have done something. How did I get in the middle of their fight?

Sabra Falling

Ismail Khalidi

Act 2. Scene 6. On the outskirts of the Sabra and Shatila refugee camps in Beirut, Lebanon. September, 1982.

During the 1982 invasion of Beirut an Israeli pilot falls through the roof of one family's home in the Palestinian refugee camp of Sabra. The heartbroken patriarch, however, confuses the pilot for his dead son, and decides to keep him in the house as the siege around the camp tightens.

Here, the daughter Dalia (20s) offers the soldiers who surround the beleaguered camp the pilot in exchange for the safety of the civilians in Sabra and Shatila who are now facing the prospect of a massacre.

DALIA: You in the tanks. I know you can hear me. I come on behalf of the people in these camps. To make a deal. There are no fighters left here. Not a kalashnikov to our names. We're defenseless… But we have one of your pilots! You withdraw and you get him back, unharmed. (*A shot rings out. Dalia ducks and then stands again.*) Where the fuck are your manners, man!? Did you not hear me? We have your man. He fell from his plane on the 11th. Look it up. (*Another shot over her head. Dalia flinches.*) We could have shot him on the spot. But we didn't. If you want, we can. We can try him for the crimes of your generals and end him right here in these alleys running with shit and blood. And I'll do it, if I have too, I will! (*The sound of laughter in the distance*) I can see you laughing. Behind all that armor! Is it because I'm a woman or because I'm not one of you that you laugh at me like a roach trapped in a jar? Hey! Let your commander hear my offer. Don't you want to go home, soldier? To your beaches and cafes modeled after Europe? Home to your mamma's cooking? You drive us from our land and make it your own, but you're not even there! It wasn't enough to chase us out and build your parks over our villages? To erase the names of places and make them your own!? Must you also follow us with your fire and metal and hunger and darkness!? (*Another shot in the air. This time Dalia does not flinch.*) I've heard how you travel once you have served your time in the army. How you take off those uniforms and put on your sandals and travel the world: Paris, India, New York, Thailand. While we are stuck here. I don't travel. I cannot. But I do know that your freedom to walk along a beach smoking hash and strumming your guitar comes at my expense, soldier. Do you hear me!? What more do you want from us? You've hunted us into the sea, blown us in bits into the sky, driven us under the earth. There is nowhere else for us to go.

Don't turn away! I may be invisible to you in the flesh but it won't be that way if I am to die at your hands tonight. You'll have no choice but to see me then, and you'll never stop seeing me. I'll follow you to Fez and Goa and to Prague. In your backpack, your pocket, among the stamps in your passport, and in the blackness when you close your eyes for the night. If you enter these camps that is what awaits. So think about it. I'm offering you a way out soldier. A way to save your man and leave. A way to take off that uniform before you find the stains too difficult to remove. And if you're in to the whole Lady Macbeth thing fine, but at least take your fucking pilot and leave us alone. You have until nightfall, soldier. Peace be with you.

The Sarimanok Travels

Francis Tanglao-Aguas

Come Forth We Men. Second Movement of this Journey of the Filipino Spirit. Present day in the backyard garden of a dilapidated home in Mountain View, California.

Filipino grandmothers, or Lolas, are the bedrock of the family. Thus, when Lola Amonita Balajadja told the world how she was terrorized as a comfort woman sex slave in World War II, Tanglao-Aguas felt it was his duty for her story to be seen like the star of the world: Estrella del Mundo. Lola Estrella may be too young to be a grandmother because her rape began when she was 12 years old, but make no mistake, she does not dwell on this, because she survived through her wit and sense of humor. In her old age she is remanded to all the housework and childcare, as her family works multiple jobs, causing them to neglect Lola Estrella.

In this monologue, Lola Estrella teaches her granddaughter, Juana, how to gain a sense of strength, pride, resilience, and indomitability. The character is female, but can be played by a man or woman.

LOLA ESTRELLA: Ampalaya* is a green and bitter fruit
that looks like the face of a two hundred year old woman.

(She subtly feels her way around the garden, making sure we do not notice that she is blind.) (*bitter melon)

Ampalaya is so bitter that my mother had to slice it so thin

so she could squeeze the bitterness away.
Yet it remained the most bitter vegetable I ever ate and I liked it.
Vitamin A for clear eyes.
Vitamin E for beautiful skin.
Vitamin C for strength against the flu.
Ampalaya is good for living.
I have not had ampalaya for twenty years or more.
I really don't know because I don't have the vitamin to remember.
I can not eat ampalaya because my granddaughter
Juana refuses to drive me to the Oriental Store in Daly City.
She is a lazy girl!
She is so lazy that once I slipped while mopping the kitchen floor
And she was on her way out the door
Why she did not even stop to help me!
She felt bad when she came home
And the neighbors were helping me
Because you see, I broke something.
She wanted to make it up to me
So I told her she knows what to do.
I was so helpful that she did know
Because she smiled at me when she left.
She came back with zucchini!
That only has Vitamin A!
It is a wimpy vegetable!
It has no power in it, only volume:
Very bland volume to use up space in your stomach.
Even a newborn infant can eat a whole zucchini!
Where I come from we don't have zucchini.
So I cooked the zucchini
With tomatoes and onions
And all the vegetables I could find.
Funny thing, this granddaughter of mine cannot eat meat.
That's why she's so weak and lazy.
That's what I'm telling you!
She ate the whole zucchini and she's still so lazy!
She cannot even help me in my garden a little bit,

Even just to talk to the vegetables.
Look at them, they are so pale and lifeless.
There are so many of them.
I cannot tell stories to all of them at the same time!
And this Juana!
Listen to her singing inside.
I tell her all the time, why not sing out here
So the vegetables can hear you?
She pretends she cannot understand Ilocano.
I don't know much English but I understand
When someone refuses to learn how to understand me.
You're listening alright,
You just don't like what you hear.
Look
Here,
This is the ampalaya plant.
It is so shameful for me to look at it.
I am so ashamed.
I am fortunate my mother is not here anymore.
What kind of woman can not grow ampalaya?
Only a lifeless woman.
(*She hears something.*)
Juana?
Juana, is that you Apo*? (*grandchild*)
If you are going to sing, Apo, sing out here.
Otherwise don't sing at all.
You are teasing my vegetables.
They will magtatampo* to your Lola. (*begrudge*)
That's why they're not growing.
How would you like it if I cooked lumpiang Shanghai
And gave them all to the Bushes next door without leaving some for you,
Ha Apo?
Apo?
Juana, my Apo, why won't you try to hear me?
I am an old woman who has no home.
Juana, can you hear me?
(*BEAT. Then…*

What follows are still English words but spelled phonetically to simulate Ilocano accented English. The "Translations" are here to guide the performer, and are NOT to be performed. There are only five vowel sounds in the Filipino languages akin to the Spanish and Japanese open vowel sounds.)

Leysee gurrl, (*Lazy girl,*)
Yu gud por nateeng gurrl. (*You good for nothing girl.*)
Elp me plunt eer! (*Help me plant here!*)

Wanna B. Amerika, yu sun up a bits... (*Juana B. Amerika, you son of a bitch...*)

Dar, wutar yurr imti ed! (*There, water your empty head!*)
(*She throws the water gourd towards the house.*)
Ay madre de puta yu leysee gurrl (*Ay! [son of a bitch] you lazy girl!*)
Sun up yurr stowpeed payrents. (*Son of your stupid parents.*)
Deed nut tits yu der on tung. (*Did not teach you their own tongue.*)
Shur is isi pur yu n pur dem (*Sure it's easy for you and for them*)
Naw dat yu tok layk gaddam Ungkool Sam. (*Now that you talk like goddamn Uncle Sam*)

Bat luk wat apend mai dotir Clarita (*But look what happened my daughter Clarita*)

Naw dat yu meyreed dat Juanito... (*Now that you married that Juanito [Hwanito]...*)

Ay told yu anak, (*I told you anak [child/daughter]*)
No kulids digri, (*No college degree,*)
No marids digri. (*No marriage degree.*)
Ay sint yu to kulids Clarita (*I sent you to college Clarita*)

Bat yu mirid dis parmer up poteyto n korn. (*But you married this farmer of potato and corn.*)

Ay don iban pid yu nating ils bat bist rays, d milagrosa. (*I don't even feed you nothing but best rice, the "miracle rice."*)

Bat istil, yu disubayd mi n mirid a parmer. (*But still, you disobeyed me and married a farmer.*)

N su yu prub mi rong jus bikos yu win ir tu Amirrika, (*And so you proved me wrong just because you went here to America.*)

Bat pur wat? Pur wat Clarita? (*But for what? For What, Clarita?*)

Yu kim ir to Amirrika to plunt d litas (*You came here to America to plant the lettuce*)

N d arrteechok n d istruberri n Wutsunbil? (*And the artichoke and the strawberry in Watsonville?*)

Di n nayt, di n nayt, yu plunt. (*Day and night, day and night, you plant.*)

N su luk wat apind tu yur dotir—(*And so look what happened to your daughter—*)

Ay kin nut plunt initing in her. (*I can not plant anything in her.*)
Dyas layk Ay kud nut in yu. (*Just like I could not in you.*)
Bat naw yu r gun (*But now you are gone*)
Wid yu asban bisayd yu (*With your husband beside you*)
Een d lan yu tild (*In the land you tilled*)
Dat olweys ridyakted yu. (*That always rejected you.*)
Haw ken yu lai dawn dir (*How can you lie down there*)

Win dis lan bamited yu in yur layp? (*When this land vomited you in your life?*)

Naw dis dotir up yurs ees bamiting mi. (*Now this daughter of yours is vomiting me.*)

Anak *[Child/Daughter]*
My anak.
I know you can hear me.
I am an old woman who has no home.

Smart People

Lydia R. Diamond

Act 1. Scene 12. Pre-Obama era. Cambridge, MA.

Valerie, (African American, anywhere between 24–28) is a recent graduate of the American Repertory Theater's MFA program. Valerie is already becoming weary of the dearth of roles for a young African American actress. She is auditioning for a role, reading from the script. She's at the climax of ghetto passion.

VALERIE: (*To table of auditors. Bag on shoulder.*) Hi. I'm Valerie Johnston and I'll be reading for (*looking at side*) Shalonda. I left my headshot with the monitor... but if you need one I...(*referencing her bag*)... O.K. then. (*She begins*)... I was lovin' you Lenny. All that time you was lookin' at me, an' I thought you was lookin' into my soul. An you wasn't seein' me at all. An I was lookin' at you, an I knowed you seed somthin. I knowed there's a man in there, an I could see him, even if you couldn't. And Mama said, she said, "naw girl, he don' love you... he only love you long as you give him what he need, stay scaret, an stay under is foot." An' I toll. I toll... (*Valerie has stopped abruptly. To casting table:*) I toll? (*working it out*) I toll her.... I toll.... OOOHhh... O.K. I told her, O.K. An I toll her she was wrong an I toll her. I got it, sorry, where should I begin? (beat) No, I can just start over. I'm so sorry, my agent didn't send the right sides, so I'm reading this cold. I was told to prepare for Mary, the social worker. Oh.... I seemed a better fit for this role... So my agent did tell you that I have a call at two. I'm doing *Enemy of the People* at the.... Sure thing.... From the top then. (beat) (*Assuming an even higher level of ghetto passion*) I was lovin' you Lenny. All that time you was lookin' at me, an' I thought you was lookin' into my soul. An' I—... Oh, Okay. Sure. Thank you...

Some People

Danny Hoch

A small apartment in 1990s New York City, but could easily be today, or a number of other cities. Blanca, a young Latina in her 20s stops by her friend Lisette's apartment before work for some chit-chat, but really to borrow some shoes.

BLANCA: Listen Lisette, lemme borrow your shoes? The short black ones. No because Manny gets off Footlocker in twenty minutes and I have to take the bus. But I can't be looking ugly in the bus. So find them! Don't stress me more alright. My life is already stressed enough, can I tell you? The other day right? I was at Manny's house, and we was fooling around, and like you know how guys be getting all shy like when they wanna say something really important but they don't say it? Or like they say it, but like their voices be getting all low so you can't hear what they saying? So he was doing that right, and like I don't be playing that. I was like, hello- excuse-me-I can't hear you-what-you-saying right?

So I figure he's doing that because he wants to ask me to marry him cause already we been together one year nine months seventeen days and he ain't asked me nothing. So I look, and he got this thing behind his back and I figure it's a Hallmark card or something saying like, hello Blanca how you doing I love you will you marry me. Instead, he got a condom right?... Right? So I was like, excuse me who's that for? He was like, that's for us. I was like, excuse me—I do not think that's for us. But he goes, no we have to use it, because he said that he had seen some thing in like channel thirteen or something, like some thing.

He goes, no you have to be careful you don't know what's out there. I was like, excuse me I know what's out there, I'm talking about what's in here, right? I was like, you ain't sticking no fucking rubber shit up inside me I don't know who touched it. You might as well put a rubber glove and do some Spic and Span in that shit, cause I ain't having that... No cause, one year nine months seventeen days we been together, *now* he comes to me with it? *Now* he thinks I'm dirty? And he thinks like I don't know nothing. Like he thought that I thought that you could get it from mosquitoes. Plus it ain't like I just met him. I know his whole family, his parents, his sisters. They're nice people. If I would have got something, I would have got it one year nine months seventeen days ago, right?... No, we talked about it but you think we used it? Ps. We started fooling around, I was like, you seen *this* in Channel Thirteen? He was like, no. I was like, mmm hmm.

...Not those, the black ones you wore last Friday! The short ones with the bows on it. I'm telling you though, Manny be driving me crazy sometimes for the dumb reasons. Like, you know Manny's father's Puerto Rican and his mother's Spanish. So he's Puerto Rican, right? And he's dark and his last name is Sorullo. So when people ask him, he always says *Sorulo.* Cause he says he wants to work in business in Wall Street, and that nobody wants to hire a Sorullo. So I be telling him, Manny that's your last name, you can't do that. And he be getting angry at me like, "That's my last name, that's how it's pronounced!" And like, "you got it easier than me Blanca cause you're lighter than me, cause you're a woman." And I'm like, excuse me, I'm Puerto Rican too, right? So it was the Puerto Rican Day Parade, and I had gotten us these T-shirts with the Puerto Rican flag in the front, and in the back there's a little Coquí and it says Boricua and Proud. So you would think that he would be like, oh thank you Blanca that's so sweet I love you, right? Instead he starts screaming. I'm not wearing this shit! I can't believe you got me this! It's ugly! I was like, excuse me, it's not ugly. So he puts on a Ralph Lauren shirt. I was like, Manny, you think somebody's hiring you for Wall Street at the Puerto Rican Day Parade? So he goes to me, Look Blanca, I might be Puerto Rican, but I don't have to walk around looking like one... I was like, excuse me. You think that people think that you're Swedish? I couldn't believe it. It's like, he wants to wear a condom, but not a T-shirt.

You got them? Finally, gimme. I hope they fit. I'm telling you, you know, what is it? But listen, I have to go because you making me late. And these shoes are too tight but I'm wearing them. And let me tell you something. If Manny comes to me with that whole condom thing again, I'm gonna tell him like this, You think I'm dirty? Who do you think I am? Do you even know who you are?

Songs of the Dragons Flying to Heaven

Young Jean Lee

Act 1. The set is a quasi-Korean-Buddhist temple. The audience spends the pre-show crowded behind the set, where an oppressively "Asian" environment has been created, complete with dragon mural, colored paper lanterns, and Asian flute music. The audience then enters the house down narrow gravel paths on either side of the temple. They sit facing the inside of the temple, which is a large, bare wooden room. In the darkness, they listen to an audio recording of Young Jean Lee rehearsing and planning a video of herself getting slapped. They then watch a video of Young Jean being slapped repeatedly in the face and crying, accompanied by a traditional Korean pansori song. When the video ends, lights come up on KOREAN AMERICAN, looking cute in a t-shirt, jeans, and sneakers. She addresses the audience, smiling.

KOREAN-AMERICAN: Have you ever noticed how most Asian-Americans are slightly brain-damaged from having grown up with Asian parents?
It's like being raised by monkeys—these retarded monkeys who can barely speak English and who are too evil to understand anything besides conformity and status. Most of us hate these monkeys from an early age and try to learn how to be human from school or television, but the result is always tainted by this subtle or not so subtle retardation. Asian people from Asia are even more brain-damaged, but in a different way, because they are the original monkey.

Anyway, some white men who like Asian women seem
to like this retarded quality as well, and sometimes the
more retarded the better.
I am so mad about all of the racist things against me
in this country, which is America.
Like the fact that the reason why so many white men
date Asian women is that they can get better-looking
Asian women than they can get white women because we
are easier to get and have lower self-esteem. It's like
going with an inferior brand so that you can afford more
luxury features. Also, Asian women will date white guys
who no white woman would touch.
But the important thing about being Korean is getting
to know your roots. Because we come to this country and
want to forget about our ancestry, but this is bad, and we
have to remember that our grandfathers and grandmothers were people too, with interesting stories to tell.
Which leads to a story from my grandmother, which is
the story of the mudfish.
In Korea they have this weird thing where everyone
turns a year older on New Year's Day. So if you were born
on December 31st, you turn one on January 1st even
though you've only been alive for a day. Anyway, each
year on New Year's Day, my grandmother used to make
this special dish called meekudaji tong that she would
only serve once a year because it was such a pain in the
ass to make.
The main ingredient of meekudaji tong is mudfish,
which are these tiny fishes they have in Korea that live
on muddy riverbanks and eat mud. Every New Year's
Day, my grandmother would throw a bunch of mudfish
into a bowl of brine, which would make them puke out all
their mud until they were shiny clean. Then she would
put pieces of tofu on a skillet, heat it up, and throw the
live mudfish onto the skillet. The mudfish would franti-
cally burrow inside the pieces of tofu to escape the heat
and, voilà, stuffed tofu!

White people are so alert to any infringement on their
rights. It's really funny. And the reason why it's funny is
that minorities have all the power. We can take the word
racism and hurl it at people and demolish them, and
there's nothing you can do to stop us.
I feel so much pity for you right now.
You have no idea what's going on. The wiliness of the
Korean is beyond anything you could ever hope to imagine.
I can promise you one thing, which is that we will
crush you.
You may laugh now, but remember my words when you
and your offspring are writhing under our yoke.
(raising her fist) Let the Korean dancing begin!

Standoff at Hwy#37

Vickie Ramirez

Act 2. Scene 5.

A Native American National Guardsman is dispatched with his unit to quell a land claim protest on contested Haudenosaunee Reservation lands. The protest takes a drastic turn when Thomas feels compelled to choose between his past—his loyalty to the Haudenosaunee people—and a promising future in the military. He has just confronted his mentor about his actions and has realized there's no way out. Sandra Henhawk (32) comforts Thomas with her own story, of how she tried to blend in outside society, but ultimately couldn't.

SANDRA: For the longest time, I tried to forget I was Mohawk. I was tired of explaining myself. Tired of the stupid questions. *Do you speak Indian? What's a sweat lodge like?* Tired of being judged by TV standards, and movie standards—you're not Indian if you don't act like an extra from Dances With Wolves.

Well, hello—I'm Haudenosaunee, Mohawk—specifically, big difference from the Lakota. We were 500 different nations—NATIONS—as in different languages and traditions—and no, I don't know what happens in a Hopi Sundance and sorry if I like to wear high heels and designer dresses occasionally. I got so tired of validating who I was to them, and tired of their presumption that their opinion mattered. Like they had the right to question us about who we are. So I stopped being Indian. I got so tired of it, I finally decided to learn Spanish, just to shut everybody up.

Then, one day the Mayor said something incredibly stupid and, I thought—racist and I couldn't get anyone to care. It felt like a punch—like a slap out of nowhere, and I didn't even realize it, but I'd started crying. So I told "my people" in the city—my friends, my ex—and they all laughed. Like it was a joke. I guess it was my fault because I'd always made jokes and laughed along in the past, because hey, "I have a sense of humor." Until I realized that nobody cared what was happening with us. I had a good job, a job that was all about selling things, making people believe things and I couldn't get anyone to buy the idea that what he said was wrong. I realized then that my job was pretty useless—who I was, was pretty useless. So I came here, and dammit if I wasn't gonna find a way to be useful. That's why I came back and that's why I started this protest—because I've played the game and ignored shit and have gone along to get along and I ended up pretty screwed. At least, here—I don't have to pretend. I can be an angry Indian, here.

Sunset Baby

Dominique Morisseau

Scene 4. An apartment in East New York. Present.

Nina, a black woman, early 20s—named after Nina Simone, is the daughter of revolutionaries. Her mother, Ashanti X, has recently passed from a drug overdose. But at one point in time, Ashanti was a powerful activist. Nina's father, Kenyatta, is a political prisoner and Black revolutionary who is recently released from prison. Abandoning the politics of her parents and their lifestyle, Nina and her boyfriend Damon "sell drugs and rob ni**as" in East New York, but Nina is growing exhausted by this criminal lifestyle. When the play opens, Kenyatta resurfaces in Nina's life in search of letters Ashanti wrote to him while he was imprisoned. Nina has inherited these letters and refuses to relinquish them to her estranged father. "Letters written to you. But left-in writing-to moi." When Damon discovers the letters, he tries to convince Nina to charge her father for them "for all those years of disappointment" so that they can escape the drug game and he can give her "the life you've been dreaming of. Lavish life." But Nina has other visions.

NINA: I'm tired, Damon. You think you more tired of these streets than me, but you ain't. I never wanted this. What I want? Something easy. I don't want a hustle or no fast money. I don't want a movement or a cause. I want a home. I want somewhere I can walk into my space and not have to look over my shoulder or hold my breath. I want some kids of my own. Lie around in a house and read 'em children's books by Camille Yarbrough or bell hooks. Learn to bake or somethin.' Have a garden and grow me some vegetables to cook and eat. Paint the living room on a Saturday. Listen to Nina (Simone) and close my eyes and sleep through the night for once in my fuckin' life. That's it. I wanna sit in the horizon somewhere and watch the sun rise and set. I never even saw a fuckin' sunset! I am not alive here. I am not alive in this chaos—you hear me? I do not want this shit no more.

The Talk

France-Luce Benson

Act 1. Scene 2. Manu's home in South Florida; the old childhood bedroom of her adult daughter. It is 3a.m.

Manu, 54, is a recently widowed, Haitian woman who immigrated to America with her husband over 20 years ago. She tried to raise her daughter, Claire, with strict, traditional Haitian-Christian values—but Claire was not having it. Consequently, their relationship has always been awkward, distant, and cold; Manu could never understand the choices Claire made. Following the death of Manu's husband, several months prior, Claire has come to help Manu settle all their affairs. When the play begins, it is Claire's last night with Manu before she returns back to her own life and home, far away from her mother. Faced with the frightening reality of being alone for the first time in her life, Manu experiences an emotional breakdown, and wakes Claire up in the middle of the night to ask her how to use a sex toy. Claire is confused, embarrassed, and furious—demanding that Manu get out and leave her alone for good. This is the key that unlocks a lifetime of emotions and desires that Manu has suppressed and unloads on her daughter.

MANU: (*Manu lets out a long, loud scream; like a caged beast screaming to be set free. Her scream should suggest years and years of repression. She stops, catches her breath, and glares at her daughter with both desperation and intimidation. After a beat, she finally speaks*)

We-Must-Have-This-Talk-Now.—Sit.—All the women in the family, your *grandmere, tanti, tous mas cousins*, all of us—we all raise the same way: <u>Don't talk about sex</u>.

When I grow up in Haiti, we don't talk about sex. Before to get married, no one talk to me about sex. When I marry your father, we have sex, but we don't talk about it. You don't talk about sex with your husband, you don't talk about sex with the children, you don't talk about sex with a friend, your pastor… You just don't talk about sex. (*beat*) You don't think about sex. If you start to think about sex, you pray. Then you take hold of those desires, and you lock them away. Somewhere far, far, far away, where not even you can find it. And you give the key to the man for safe keeping. It is his job to protect it. It is the man's job to protect what is sacred, and forbidden. That is what we call <u>mystique</u>. It is the way I was raised. I try to raise you in the same way. *Bon Dieu, Jesi, Mary, Joseph*, how hard I try with you. But you and your American ways. You never listen to me; DRESS like I don't know what. Speak to me any way you like. And the way you live your life? Leaving home at seventeen. Seventeen! "It is good," everyone say. "She go to school. She go to a good school. The best school." But Claire, for seven years? Seven years. Seven years in school! And now?—You do Yoga.

The Trajectory of a Heart, Fractured

Sung Rno

Scene 4. A street corner in a city that could be New York City, but then again could not.

Joanne is an Asian American woman, 40ish although she seems younger; she is at that age when regret is starting to infuse much of her life. Joanne and Orville meet in an airport over a Polaroid camera, and find that their relationship is always developing, coming and going, and slightly up in the air. Their history is so turbulent that it becomes unclear what actually happened, what is imagined, and what are outright lies. Ultimately, their love fractures and Orville ends up with someone else who is totally not right for him, Yumi, and they fly to Asia together. Tragically, this plane disappears over the Pacific Ocean. Right before Orville got on the plane, he bumped into Joanne on the street. Having just learned the news of the lost plane, Joanne stares up at the sky, drinking a bad cup of deli coffee.

In this monologue she traces the history of her feelings for Orville, with all the joys and regrets of seeing him again.

JOANNE: I told him I was happily married with 2 kids. I don't. And I'm not. I'm actually going through a divorce. I'm not sure why I lied to him. Maybe cuz he looked so damn happy. I didn't want him to feel sorry for me. We were on the street and he asked me if I wanted to get a cup of coffee. I said, sure, I just had ten minutes before I had to be somewhere. We stopped by this deli and we got 2 cups of coffee. The coffee was awful.

I heard about it on the news. They still don't know what really happened. Some people think it was a terrorist. Others think it was the weather. I heard some people talking about wind shear. Wind shear. Like what the hell is that?

Now, I'm thinking why did I lie to him? I wonder if he was thinking of me at all up there in the sky? Don't look at me like that. It's not like you're any better. Or you. Yeah, you.

When I heard the news I didn't know what to do. Or where to go. It's not like anyone would really understand the feelings I'm going through. I want to throw up, punch my hand through a window. I want to break the moon across someone's head.

So I go back to that deli and order a cup of that black coffee. It's so black that it's bending the surrounding light into the cup. I stand on the street sipping. Ugh. That coffee is like acid. It melts a hole through my stomach. My insides slowly ooze out of this hole and drip onto the sidewalk. The coffee is burning a bigger and bigger hole in me. But I like the awful way it tastes. I stare up at the sky. And I take. One. More. Long. Sip.

Twilight

Anna Deavere Smith

"Swallowing the Bitterness" Mrs. Young Soon-Han

Anna Deavere Smith's one woman play *Twilight* utilizes interview theater techniques to probe conflicts or themes within a specific community. *Twilight* examines the turbulent aftermath of the 1992 Rodney King trial, verdict and riots in Los Angeles. In the last section of the play, entitled "Justice" she examines the diverse reactions of the white, Korean, Latin and African American communities as they each struggle to return to normalcy post-verdict and hope for a better American future.

The setting for this interview is Los Angeles. 1992. "A house on Sycamore Street just south of Beverly. A tree-lined street. A quiet street. It's an area where many Hasidic Jews live as well as yuppie types. Mrs. Young Soon-Han's living room is impeccable… She sits on the floor leaning on the coffee table."

In this verbatim account, Mrs. Young Soon-Han, a former liquor store owner, describes how she must "swallow the bitterness" she feels regarding the Rodney King verdict, and yearns for equal acknowledgement of Korean American suffering in the midst of the turmoil caused by the riots.

MRS YOUNG SOON-HAN: Until last year
I believed America is the best.
I still believe it.
I don't deny that now.
Because I'm victim.

But
as
the year ends in ninety-two,
and we were still in turmoil,
and having all the financial problems,
and mental problems,
then a couple months ago,
I really realized that
Korean immigrants were left out
from this
society and we were nothing.
What is our right?
Is it because we are Korean?
Is it because we have no politicians?
Is it because we don't
speak good English?
Why?
Why do we have to be left out?
(*She is hitting her hand on the coffee table.*)
We are not qualified to have medical treatment!
We are not qualified to get uh
food stamps!
(*She hits the table once.*)
No GR!
(*Hits the table once.*)
Anything!
Many Afro-Americans
(*Two quick hits.*)
who never worked
(*One hit.*)
they get
at least minimum amount
(*One hit.*)
of money
(*One hit.*)
to survive!

(*One hit.*)
We don't get any!
(*Large hit with full hand spread.*)
Because we have a *car!*
(*One hit.*)
and we have a *house!*
(*Pause six seconds.*)
And we are *high tax payers!*
(*One hit.*)
(*Pause fourteen seconds.*)
Where do I finda [*sic*] justice?
Okay, black people
Probably,
believe they won
by the trial?
Even some complains only half, right
justice was there?
But I watched the television
that Sunday morning
Early morning as they started
I started watch it all day.
They were having party, and then they celebrated (*Pronounced CeLEbreted.*)
all of South Central,
all the churches,
they finally found that justice exists
in this society.
Then where is the victims' rights?
They got their rights
by destroying *innocent Korean merchants* (*Louder.*)
They have a lot of respect, (*Softer*)
as I do
for Dr. Martin King?
He is the only model for black community.
I don't care Jesse Jackson.
But,
he was the model

of non-violence
Non-violence?
They like to have hiseh [sic] spirits.
What about last year?
They destroyed innocent people!
(*Five second pause.*)
And I wonder if that is really justice,
(*And a very soft uh after justice like justicah, but very quick.*)
to get their rights
in this way.
(*Thirteen second pause.*)
I waseh swallowing the bitternesseh.
Sitting here alone, and watching them.
They became all hilarious.
(*Three second pause.*)
And uh,
in a way I was happy for them,
and I felt glad for them,
at least they got something back, you know.
Just lets forget Korean victims or other victims
who are destroyed by them.
They have fought
for their rights
(*One hit simultaneous with the word rights.*)
over two centuries
(*One hit simultaneous with centuries.*)
and I have a lot of sympathy and understanding for them.
Because of their effort, and understanding,
other minorities like And Hispanic
or Asians
maybe we have to suffer more
by mainstream,
you know?
That's why I understand.
And then
I like to be part of their

joyment.
But.
That's why I had mixed feeling
as soon as I heard the verdict.
I wish I could
live together
with eh [sic] blacks
but after the riots
there were too much differences
The fire is still there
how do you call it
(*She says a Korean word asking for translation. In Korean she says "igniting fire."*)
igni
igniting fire
It canuh
burst out any time.

Wings of Night Sky, Wings of Morning Light

Joy Harjo

Act 1. Scene 12. Indian Arts Boarding School, Santa Fe, New Mexico, 1967

Redbird Monahwee is a Muscogee Creek teenager, 15, who has escaped to Indian boarding school to save her life from harassment by a step-father, and to further her studies in painting. She has been kept in the dorm on a Friday night with other female students who are on restriction for various infractions, mostly drinking. The irony is that it is easier to get alcohol while on restriction because other students feel sorry for those who can't come out and party. She is pretty lit at the top of the monologue. She is usually very shy but is loosened up by the hard stuff as she speaks with the other girls on restriction.

In this monologue, the Spirit Helper has told Redbird that in order to heal from a drunken car wreck, where she is now suspended in a coma between life and death, she has to go back through the whole story, to reclaim pieces of her lost soul.

REDBIRD: (*Drunk*) I call to order the meeting of girls on restriction at Indian school. We broke the rules. Now we're locked up in the dorm on Saturday night. "Where's the dorm matron? Break out the stash. Let's dance."

We all admire Marlene; she's one of the best. She's Jackson Pollack in a dress. She only leaves the painting studio for sleep or work, and on Sunday she sneaks out to the Indian hospital on the other side of campus. She took me once. The children clapped and laughed when she came in. She brought them gifts: crayons, paper, tiny fans, all her desserts saved up for a week. When the staff came in, we hid. They eventually threw her out. The hospital carried no insurance to cover the harm she might do. Here's to you Marlene!

And Venus Ramierez, now that's a name, and a history: one parent from the north on the back of a horse, the other from the south over the back of a river. Venus is a singer, a real singer. Each singer has a particular gift. Some grow plants, some call helpers. Some heal the sick, some make the dead rise up and dance. When Venus sings we enter into a trance. We no longer hurt from freak chance. You're going to make it to Broadway
Either New York or Albuquerque!
None of us are coping well with the Bureau of Indian Affairs.
We've read the reports: "Doesn't play well with others", "won't speak or look us in the eyes", "talks to ghosts."
We hear what they are really saying: "We have the guns and money, and we have your children."
Where's Kit? We can't find Kit anywhere.
She's not in the laundry room, practicing powwow in her underwear. She's not out on the roof where she sneaks her smokes. She's not in the tent she made of government issued bedspreads, where she sketches high fashion of Indians in Paris.
Here comes Kit with a knife. And there she goes. No top or bottom, only fury whirling in a spiritual nudity.
She's headed out into the snow.
She's what happens when someone hurts the baby.
My escape to Indian school was a success.
I present myself as case in point. I can corner my sheets so a quarter spins, and knows the drill for shots, debugging and towels. And because I've forgotten the Indian language I learned in the cradle, I have a chance. If I let them suck out my soul and put it in the closet with my ancestors' bones—I'll make it.

The Women of Tu-Na House

Nancy Eng

Act 1. Scene 6. Employee locker room of Asian massage parlor in New York City, May 2010.

Patrons get "more bang for a buck" at Tu-Na House if "...know who to request." But take who they can get at their own risk while legit business expands. Kind-hearted "pseudo" Madam lets women employed choose what to do, don't do, or pretend to be as she operates licensed "*Tu-Na*" parlor to pay forward "own happy ending" she inherited from former John. Offers of "...welcome *dissycount*" or "...ten *dolla* for ten *minie*" or "*haff-our* only twenty-*fie*..." chair massages. She solicits mostly non-Asian pedestrians outside her brownstone near the United Nations and invites them on impromptu tours before meeting Mei-Li Lu—the filial Chinese daughter born to an illustrious clan from the province of Hunan but raised in a poor village after the ancestor's fall from grace. She earns money as Masseuse #42 to rebuild the denounced village with her dignity rebuilt by the family's restored honor. Potential patrons encounter her, aged well in her 40s, as she begins to change clothes after elderly *Tea Lady* has left the kitchen with more tea for patrons touring the employee lounge.

In this monologue, Mei-Li tells her own struggle for survival as she puts on appropriate work attire and proudly reveals secret of her success before leaving to start her shift.

MEI-LI: (*Speaks w/slight Mandarin accent*) When I was young, there use to be a festival held in honor of one of the villagers who passed the

Imperial exam to become a magistrate of the court. Each year on his lunar birthday, everyone line up to pray for health, wealth and prosperity at statue with his name, "Lu Wei-Hu, the smartest man in Lu Village." But that was then, now he is called Lu The Fool, imperialistic running donkey of the Ching Dynasty, stupid asshole for short. (*Puts on high heel shoes*) Stupid asshole did not foresee his former glory would result in the denouncement and disgrace of entire village during the Cultural Revolution. Village lucky only had to pay heavy fine and was only partially destroyed. Village was lucky no one taken away or hurt. But village be more lucky if stupid asshole was born a stupid asshole. I, no such luck. Belong to family direct descendant of stupid asshole, blamed for downfall and burdened with responsibility too. Reason why I was sent to earn more money in Shanghai to help rebuild village when I grew up. But like every country girl in the big city with no skills or the proper-papers, I had to become a chicken in order to eat. (*Walks across in high heels.*) *Swor-gee, jou-guy...*you know? Not the kind they fry in Kentucky. I talking about kind that walk across road to get to lonely man on the other side. Maybe why hooker in China called chicken. Cross the road, get it? Never mind. One day man asks me to work at his restaurant in NY and offer good pay. But then I think to myself and got mad. Stupid come here to find worker. Not enough Chinese in New York? Told him no can work in restaurant make money if I not owner unless...chicken only thing on the menu. He laugh, say I smart. Promise me easy money if I follow...so I follow. Work for stupid asshole three years just to pay for passage but now I work here...for myself (*Puts on smock*). Finally make enough money to sent and spend. First time I so happy save for trip back home but not to see village. Everybody smile to my face but laugh behind me. My family was so ashamed by how I was treated. On way to airport when time to leave, they told me "No have to come back see us. We understand. Just send money. Inside we know you still good daughter." I just nodded my head but my eyes began to fill with tears once I sat on the airplane. Then I started to think and got mad. The more I think, the madder I got. Plane ride 18 hours, that a lot of time to think! By the time I got home, I was so angry and rush to call village. Village only have one phone then, always on speaker so everyone can hear. "Wai, tuen-jeung? Just want to call you as the village head and thank everyone for their warm hospitality..." I hear them snicker so talk louder. "...by buying a 70" LCD flat screen TV for the

Community Center but..." Suddenly I hear people cheer and clap in the background before someone finally thank me and then I made sure they all heard. "Only for my family to watch! No need for you to waste on rest of villagers if they can look at me and see shit for free. Unless better I spend my money on me than village." The next time I came to visit, they held a huge banquet in my honor. Everybody came, even the provincial mayor. Lucky I don't visit as often as I used to or else they'd be wasting all my money on me. Customer tell me, you can be legal chicken in Reno, Las Vegas. So one holiday I go see. Now three times a year for two weeks, I work at the Happy Hopping Blue Bunny Brothel off route 69. Owner promote me as special event, "Celestial Delight, have a taste and in one hour you're hungry for more." Make a lot of money, I so busy. Always fully book. Owner ask me why I not stay. Ever eat the Chinese food in Vegas? Taste like shit. Starve to death in no time if I have no time to cook! He laugh, say better I not stay, can still promote me as special event. Lose weight every time I come back, tell everybody I went to spa instead. Don't want anybody here know where I go, what I do or maybe they get same idea. Just another chicken in the coop if they do too. Everybody know men are cheap but stupid assholes don't mind paying more if they think it will get them something special. Shhh...

The World of Extreme Happiness

Frances Ya-Chu Cowhig

Act 1. Scene 8. The Great Hall of the People. Beijing, China. 2012.

Sunny is a 19 year-old Chinese peasant-turned-factory girl. She's been working as a janitor at Jade River Manufacturing in Shenzhen for the past four years. She has been selected by the factory management to be the 'model peasant' introducing a propagandistic pseudo-documentary, 'Factory Girl,' a PR event designed to rehabilitate the public image of the factory after a string of worker suicides. During the speech, Sunny goes off-script and decides to use the opportunity to advocate for real change.

SUNNY: (*Into microphone*) Ladies and gentlemen, esteemed foreigners, press and business people—Good morning. My name is Sunny Li, and I am here to tell you how leaving the countryside to work in a city factory gave me the—the opportunity to—to transform my life and have—. To have—To have some Success. Success. Back home—ummm…back home it was—it was my job to grow food. Mostly vegetables. I was a bad farmer. My plants got sick. They dried up—or got moldy. And eaten—by stink bugs, and grasshoppers. They didn't—they didn't grow the way vegetables should. My neighbor caught me yelling at my vegetables. She told me to stop being an idiot, brought over a wheelbarrow full of manure, and taught me how to feed vegetables—and surround them with straw—so they wouldn't burn in hot weather—or freeze in the winter. Then I went to Shenzhen. To the factory. And…and I didn't like—I hated who I was. I thought the problem was me. I needed to change—so I did. I went to night school—and studied self-improvement. I put marbles in my mouth.

Bleach on my skin. Books on my head. Every month I tried a new hair color. One day—I was walking past a building covered in shiny windows, and saw the reflection of a city girl in it. It was me! Then two people from Beijing asked me for directions—they thought I was a city person—like them. That night I went to the top floor of a department store, got eyelash extensions and ate a hamburger in the food court. It felt like the beginning of success—even city people thought I was one of them. I didn't know it wouldn't matter how much I looked like a city person— or how many people I tricked, because my ID card said peasant. City people. They think they can burn through peasants. Like a—a natural resource. To them we're coal. We don't have the same rights, but…. But we're supposed to make them rich. I want to say, to the other migrants, that I am sorry for trying to be different. I thought—I thought it was the only way I could—save myself. And change my destiny. But destiny—it's not something one person can change. We have to work together and make—better growing conditions. For all of us. We need to have better dreams. My section manager jumped out a factory window. There was a—petition by his body. Filled with hundreds of signatures. Every name was a protest. In the countryside there are always reasons to protest and people telling you not to protest. I want to say—to all my fellow migrant workers who are watching me right now—that I protest—and I ask you to protest with me. Ask—demand that you…that you get the same rights as people born in the city. If they say no… go on strike. Stop working. Make these demands every day—for a month. And—and if they still say no…if they still say no—go home. Let city people—try to live—for a single day without us. Stop selling them food and digging out coal. Stop building their houses and sewing their clothes. Let the city people go hungry. Let them…walk—naked. On the street. Without shoes. And live in houses with—with broken windows and—(*Lights shift. Sunny is alone backstage, more grounded and sure of herself than ever.*) (*Dreamy*) Cut off my head—I can still strike. Cut off my legs—I can still walk. Rip out my heart—I will mysteriously recover. I can bathe in boiling oil and come out cleaner than I went in.